# SCHOLASTIC
## LITERACY SKILLS

# Grammar and punctuation
## Year 5

## TERMS AND CONDITIONS

### IMPORTANT – PERMITTED USE AND WARNINGS – READ CAREFULLY BEFORE USING

**Minimum system requirements:**

- PC or Mac with CD-ROM drive (16x speed recommended) and 512MB RAM
- P4 or G4 processor
- Windows 2000/XP/Vista or Mac OSX 10.3 or later

For all technical support queries, please phone Scholastic Customer Services on 0845 6039091.

**Author**

Huw Thomas

**Editor**

Rachel Mackinnon

**Assistant editors**

Vicky Butt and Louise Titley

**CD-ROM design and development team**

Joy Monkhouse, Anna Oliwa,
Micky Pledge, Rebecca Male, Allison Parry,
Haremi and Q&D Multimedia Ltd

**Series designers**

Shelley Best and Anna Oliwa

**Book design team**

Shelley Best and Sonja Bagley

**Illustrations**

Moreno Chiacchiera/Beehive Illustration

Designed using Adobe Indesign
Published by Scholastic Ltd,
Book End, Range Road, Witney,
Oxfordshire OX29 0YD
www.scholastic.co.uk

Printed by Bell & Bain Ltd, Glasgow
Text © 1999, 2008 Huw Thomas
© 2008 Scholastic Ltd
2 3 4 5 6 7 8 9 0   0 1 2 3 4 5 6 7

**British Library Cataloguing-in-Publication Data**
A catalogue record for this book is available from
the British Library.
**ISBN 978-1407-10048-7**

**Mixed Sources**
Product group from well-managed
forests and other controlled sources
www.fsc.org  Cert no. TT-COC-002769
© 1996 Forest Stewardship Council

## Acknowledgements

The publishers gratefully acknowledge permission to reproduce
the following copyright material:

**Anova Books** for the use of 'Three Raindrops' from *Fairy Tales* by
Terry Jones © 1981, Terry Jones (1981, Pavilion Books).
**Faber and Faber Ltd** for the use of 'The Great Querne' from *The
Rollickers and other Stories* by Andrew Gibson © 1992, Andrew
Gibson (1992, Faber and Faber).
**A M Heath & Co Ltd** for the use of an extract from *The Ghost
Drum* by Susan Price © 1990, Susan Price (1989, Faber and Faber).
**Penguin Group (UK)** for use of an extract from *Kasper in the
Glitter* by Philip Ridley © 1994, Philip Ridley (1994, Viking, 1995
Puffin Books)
**Peters Fraser and Dunlop Ltd** for the use of the poem 'Busy Day'
by Michael Rosen from *You Tell Me* by Michael Rosen © 1981,
Michael Rosen (1981, Puffin) and the poem 'Don't' by Michael
Rosen from *Don't put mustard in the custard* by Michael Rosen ©
1985, Michael Rosen (1985, Andre Deutsch).
**Taylor and Francis Group Ltd** for the use of 'They are playing
a game' and 'I want it' by R D Laing © 1972, R D Laing (1972,
Routledge).
**A P Watt Ltd** for extracts from *Kasper in the Glitter* by Philip Ridley
© 1994, Philip Ridley (1994 Viking, 1995 Puffin Books).

Every effort has been made to trace copyright holders for the
works reproduced in this book, and the publishers apologise for
any inadvertent omissions.

Extracts from Primary National Strategy's Primary Framework for
Literacy (2006) www.standards.dfes.gov.uk/primaryframework ©
Crown copyright. Reproduced under the terms of the Click Use
Licence.

# Contents

INTRODUCTION .................................................................... 4

FRAMEWORK OBJECTIVES ................................................ 7

## Chapter 1
### Verbs

INTRODUCTION .........................................9

VERBS ....................................................12

AUXILIARY VERBS..................................16

VERB FORMS...........................................20

PERSON...................................................24

VERBS IN WRITING.................................28

## Chapter 2
### Pronouns and nouns

INTRODUCTION ................................................. 32

NOUN SORTS ..................................................... 35

THE FUNCTION OF PRONOUNS ....................... 39

NOUN AND PRONOUN PLAY ............................ 43

APOSTROPHE OF POSSESSION....................... 47

NOUNS, PRONOUNS AND WRITING................. 51

## Chapter 3
### Clauses

INTRODUCTION .....................................55

MAIN CLAUSES ....................................58

CLAUSES IN SENTENCES.....................62

CONNECTIVES......................................66

USING CONNECTIVES ..........................70

EXPERIMENTING WITH CLAUSES

IN WRITING...........................................74

## Chapter 4
### Prepositions and punctuation

INTRODUCTION ................................................. 78

INTRODUCING PREPOSITIONS ......................... 81

UNDERSTANDING PREPOSITIONS .................... 85

USING PREPOSITIONS ....................................... 89

WORD ORDER.................................................... 93

WRITING PREPOSITIONS .................................. 97

## Chapter 5
### Long and short sentences

INTRODUCTION......................................101

SENTENCE CONSTRUCTION..................104

PUNCTUATION......................................108

EMBEDDED CLAUSES AND

COMMAS ..........................................112

PUNCTUATING COMPLEX

SENTENCES ............................116

CRAFTING SENTENCES

IN WRITING......................120

## Chapter 6
### Sentences and readers

INTRODUCTION ............................................... 124

SPEECH AND WRITING ..................................... 127

DIRECT AND REPORTED SPEECH ..................... 131

READER GUIDES .............................................. 135

AUDIENCES AND SENTENCES.......................... 139

WRITING SPEECH............................................. 143


SUBJECT KNOWLEDGE ...................................... 147

# Introduction

### The Scholastic Literacy Skills: Grammar and punctuation series

This series works from the premise that grammar and punctuation can be interesting and dynamic – but on one condition. The condition is that the teaching of these aspects of grammar must be related to real texts and practical activities that experiment with language, investigate the use of language in real contexts and find the ways in which grammar and punctuation are used in our day-to-day talk, writing and reading. This book encourages children to look back at their written work and find ways to revise and improve it.

### Teaching grammar and punctuation

'As a writer I know that I must select studiously the nouns, pronouns, verbs, adverbs, etcetera, and by a careful syntactical arrangement make readers laugh, reflect or riot.'
Maya Angelou

The *Scholastic Literacy Skills: Grammar and punctuation* series equips teachers with resources and subject training enabling them to teach grammar and punctuation. The focus of the resource is on what is sometimes called sentence-level work, so called because grammar and punctuation primarily involve the construction and understanding of sentences.

Many teachers bring with them a lot of past memories when they approach the teaching of grammar. Some will remember school grammar lessons as the driest of subjects, involving drills and parsing, and will wonder how they can make it exciting for their own class. At the other end of the spectrum, some will have received relatively little formal teaching of grammar at school. In other words, there are teachers who, when asked to teach clause structure or prepositions, feel at a bit of a loss. They are being asked to teach things they are not confident with themselves. Even worse, they think they should be confident in these things.

Grammar can evoke lethargy, fear, irritation, pedantry and despondency. Yet as can be seen from the above comment by Maya Angelou, we have one of the greatest modern writers presenting her crafting of sentences as an exciting and tactical process that has a powerful effect on her readers. Can this be the grammar that makes teachers squirm or run?

### About the product

The book is divided into six chapters. Each chapter looks at a different aspect of grammar and punctuation and is divided into five sections. Each section includes teachers' notes – objective, background knowledge, notes on how to use the photocopiable pages, further ideas and what's on the CD-ROM – and two to three photocopiable pages.

### Posters

Each chapter has two posters. These posters are related to the contents of the chapter and should be displayed and used for reference throughout the work on the chapter. The poster notes (on the chapter opening page) offer suggestions for how they could be used. There are black and white versions in the book and full-colour versions on the CD-ROM for you to print out or display on your whiteboard.

### Activities

Each section contains two to three activities. These activities all take the form of a photocopiable page which is in the book. Each photocopiable page is also included on the CD-ROM for you to display or print out (these pages also provide answers where appropriate). Over thirty of the photocopiable pages have linked interactive activities on the CD-ROM. These interactive activities are designed to act as starter activities to the lesson, giving whole-class support on the information being taught. However, they can also work equally well as plenary activities, reviewing the work the children have just completed.

## Writing sections

The final section in each chapter focuses on writing. It differs slightly in layout to the other sections – rather than teaching children new skills, you are encouraging them to practise the ones they have already learned throughout the chapter and to use them in writing. There are two photocopiable pages in each of these sections; many of them are writing frames or provide prompts to encourage the children to write. As with the other sections, a number of further ideas are also included, which provide imaginative and interesting starting points for writing.

## Using the CD-ROM

Below are brief guidance notes for using the CD-ROM. For more detailed information, see **How to use** on the start-up screen, or **Help** on the relevant screen for information about that page.

The CD-ROM follows the structure of the book and contains:

- All of the photocopiable pages.
- All of the poster pages in full colour.
- Photocopiable pages (with answers where appropriate).
- Over thirty interactive on-screen activities linked to the photocopiable pages.

## Getting started

To begin using the CD-ROM, simply place it in your CD- or DVD-ROM drive. Although the CD-ROM should auto-run, if it fails to do so, navigate to the drive and double-click on the red **Start** icon.

## Start-up screen

The start-up screen is the first screen that appears. Here you can access: terms and conditions, registration links, how to use the CD-ROM and credits. If you agree to the terms and conditions, click **Start** to continue.

## Main menu

The main menu provides links to all of the chapters or all of the resources. Clicking on the relevant **Chapter** icon will take you to the chapter screen where you can access the posters and the chapter's sections. Clicking on **All resources** will take you to a list of all the resources, where you can search by key word or chapter for a specific resource.

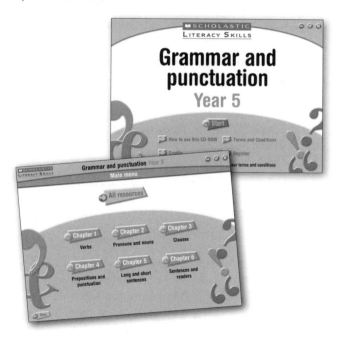

### Section screen

Upon choosing a section from the chapter screen, you are taken to a list of resources for that section. Here you can access all of the photocopiable pages related to that section as well as the linked interactive activities.

### Resource finder

The **Resource finder** lists all of the resources on the CD-ROM. You can:

- Select a chapter and/or section by selecting the appropriate title from the drop-down menus.
- Search for key words by typing them into the search box.
- Scroll up or down the list of resources to locate the required resource.
- To launch a resource, simply click on its row on the screen.

### Navigation

The resources (poster pages, photocopiable pages and interactive activities) all open in separate windows on top of the menu screen. This means that you can have more than one resource open at the same time. To close a resource, click on the **x** in the top right-hand corner of the screen. To return to the menu screen you can either close or minimise a resource.

Closing a resource will not close the program. However, if you are in a menu screen, then clicking on the **x** will close the program. To return to a previous menu screen, you need to click on the **Back** button.

### Glossary

Most of the interactive activities link to a glossary. The glossary will open in a separate window. Simply click first on the desired headletter and then on the word to reveal its definition.

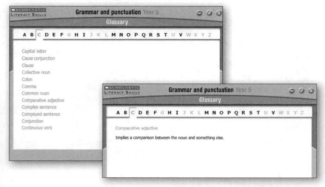

### Whiteboard tools

The CD-ROM comes with its own set of whiteboard tools for use on any whiteboard. These include:

- Pen tool
- Highlighter tool
- Eraser
- Sticky note

Click on the **Tools** button at the foot of the screen to access these tools.

### Printing

Print the resources by clicking on the **Print** button. The photocopiable pages print as full A4 portrait pages, but please note if you have a landscape photocopiable page or poster you need to set the orientation to landscape in your print preferences. The interactive activities will print what is on the screen. For a full A4 printout you need to set the orientation to landscape in your print preferences.

# Framework objectives

| Page | Section | Literacy skills objective | Strand 6: Group and classify words according to their spelling patterns and their meanings. | Strand 7: Explore how writers use language for comic and dramatic effects. | Strand 8: Compare how a common theme is presented in poetry, prose and other media. | Strand 9: Reflect independently and critically on their own writing and edit and improve it. | Strand 9: Experiment with different narrative forms and styles to write their own stories. | Strand 11: Adapt sentence construction to different text-types, purposes and readers. | Strand 11: Punctuate sentences accurately, including using speech marks and apostrophes. |
|---|---|---|---|---|---|---|---|---|---|
| 12 | Verbs | Revise work on verbs. | | | | | ✓ | | |
| 16 | Auxiliary verbs | Understand the term 'auxiliary verb'. | ✓ | ✓ | | | | | |
| 20 | Verb forms | Examine the forms of verbs in different types of sentence. | | ✓ | | | ✓ | | |
| 24 | Person | Identify and experiment with person in verbs. | | | | | ✓ | ✓ | |
| 28 | Verbs in writing | Develop the use of verbs in writing. | | | | | ✓ | ✓ | |
| 35 | Noun sorts | Revisit the different types of noun. | ✓ | ✓ | | | ✓ | ✓ | |
| 39 | The function of pronouns | Revise the function of pronouns. | | ✓ | | | | | |
| 43 | Noun and pronoun play | Investigate the function of pronouns and their reference. | | | ✓ | | | | |
| 47 | Apostrophe of possession | Revise the use of the apostrophe for possession. | | | | ✓ | | | ✓ |
| 51 | Nouns, pronouns and writing | Develop the use of nouns and pronouns in writing. | | | | | ✓ | ✓ | |
| 58 | Main clauses | Identify the main clause in a sentence. | | ✓ | | | ✓ | ✓ | |
| 62 | Clauses in sentences | Investigate sentences that contain more than one clause. | | | | ✓ | ✓ | ✓ | ✓ |
| 66 | Connectives | Understand how clauses are connected. | ✓ | | | | ✓ | ✓ | |
| 70 | Using connectives | Use connectives to link clauses and sentences. | ✓ | ✓ | | | ✓ | ✓ | |
| 74 | Experimenting with clauses in writing | Apply learning about clauses to writing. | | | | | ✓ | ✓ | |

Chapter 1 — pages 12–28
Chapter 2 — pages 35–51
Chapter 3 — pages 58–74

# Framework objectives

| Chapter | Page | Section | Literacy skills objective | Strand 6: Group and classify words according to their spelling patterns and their meanings. | Strand 7: Explore how writers use language for comic and dramatic effects. | Strand 8: Compare how a common theme is presented in poetry, prose and other media. | Strand 9: Reflect independently and critically on their own writing and edit and improve it. | Strand 9: Experiment with different narrative forms and styles to write their own stories. | Strand 11: Adapt sentence construction to different text types, purposes and readers. | Strand 11: Punctuate sentences accurately, including using speech marks and apostrophes. |
|---|---|---|---|---|---|---|---|---|---|---|
| Chapter 4 | 81 | Introducing prepositions | Identify prepositions. | ✓ | ✓ | | | | | |
| Chapter 4 | 85 | Understanding prepositions | Experiment with a range of prepositions. | | | | | | | |
| Chapter 4 | 89 | Using prepositions | Experiment with the use of prepositions. | | ✓ | | | ✓ | | |
| Chapter 4 | 93 | Word order | Investigate word order and key words, looking at the alteration of sentences. | | | | ✓ | ✓ | ✓ | |
| Chapter 4 | 97 | Writing prepositions | Use a range of prepositions to enhance precision in writing. | | | | | ✓ | ✓ | |
| Chapter 5 | 104 | Sentence construction | Construct sentences in different ways. | | | | | | ✓ | ✓ |
| Chapter 5 | 108 | Punctuation | Use punctuation in longer, more complex sentences. | | | | | | ✓ | ✓ |
| Chapter 5 | 112 | Embedded clauses and commas | Secure the use of the comma in embedding clauses within sentences. | | | | ✓ | | ✓ | ✓ |
| Chapter 5 | 116 | Punctuating complex sentences | Use punctuation marks accurately in complex sentences. | | | | | | ✓ | ✓ |
| Chapter 5 | 120 | Crafting sentences in writing | Apply clause structure and punctuation in writing. | | | | ✓ | ✓ | ✓ | ✓ |
| Chapter 6 | 127 | Speech and writing | Investigate the difference between spoken and written language. | | | ✓ | | | | ✓ |
| Chapter 6 | 131 | Direct and reported speech | Understand the difference between direct and reported speech. | | | ✓ | | | | ✓ |
| Chapter 6 | 135 | Reader guides | Understand the ways in which punctuation and the setting out of dialogue aid the reader. | | ✓ | | | | ✓ | ✓ |
| Chapter 6 | 139 | Audiences and sentences | Review and edit sentences with reference to the audience of a text. | | | ✓ | | | ✓ | ✓ |
| Chapter 6 | 143 | Writing speech | Accurately and imaginatively present speech in writing. | | | | | ✓ | | ✓ |

# Chapter 1

# Verbs

## Introduction

Verbs are those all-important words that are needed in the vast majority of sentences. In this chapter children extend their understanding of verbs through activities that examine the form and person of verbs. There is also an introduction to auxiliary verbs. This is crucial because some of the verbs children are most familiar with, such as 'can' and 'do', are auxiliaries.

## Poster notes

**Sentence types (page 10)**
This poster presents the four types of sentence and will support work on verbs in 'Person' (page 24).

**Words that make auxiliary verbs (page 11)**
This poster presents a few of the words that function as auxiliary verbs with examples of this function. As such it supports each of the units on auxiliaries. It should be stressed that these are a few examples and that other auxiliaries are encountered in the activities.

## In this chapter

| | |
|---|---|
| **Verbs** page 12 | Revise work on verbs. |
| **Auxiliary verbs** page 16 | Understand the term 'auxiliary verb'. |
| **Verb forms** page 20 | Examine the forms of verbs in different types of sentence. |
| **Person** page 24 | Identify and experiment with person in verbs. |
| **Verbs in writing** page 28 | Develop the use of verbs in writing. |

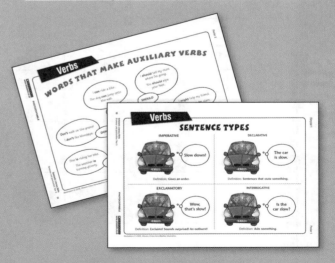

# Verbs

# SENTENCE TYPES

**DECLARATIVE**

The car is slow.

Definition: **Sentences that state something.**

**INTERROGATIVE**

Is the car slow?

Definition: **Asks something.**

**IMPERATIVE**

Slow down!

Definition: **Gives an order.**

**EXCLAMATORY**

Wow, that's slow!

Definition: **Exclaims! Sounds surprised! An outburst!**

*Illustrations © 2008, Moreno Chiacchiera/Beehive Illustration.*

# Verbs

Revise work on verbs.

## Background knowledge

Verbs are words that denote an action or happening in a sentence. They can be:

● **Active:** denoting an action actively done *by* someone or something – for example, *The boy kicked the ball through the window*, or *The wind blew the tree over.*

● **Passive:** denoting an action done *to* someone or something – for example, *The ball was kicked through the window* or *The tree was blown over by the wind.*

The subject of a verb is sometimes called the 'agent'. This denotes the person or thing that performs the action, so in both the 'blown' and 'blew' examples above the wind is the subject of the verb.

## Activities

These activities revise the idea of a verb and look at the tenses and subjects of various verbs. The terms 'subject' and 'tense' are used in the activities and the teacher is encouraged to use them with the class.

● **Photocopiable page 13 'Odd happenings'**
The odd occurrences in these text extracts provide interesting settings for unusual happenings, such as a person barking and a cat telling stories. These are analysed as children look at the verbs. The activity can begin with the children reading the texts and circling the verbs they encounter before completing the table.

● **Photocopiable page 14 'Changing tenses'**
As children remodel language from one tense to another two useful strategies are, firstly to say the sentence aloud and remodel it in speech before writing it down; and secondly, it helps if they think of the present tense sentence as happening 'today' and the past tense

sentence as happening 'yesterday'. These words tend to provide a useful way of focusing the language in the past or present.

● **Photocopiable page 15 'Verb table'**
The analysis of verbs encouraged by this table should lead to some interesting readings of various texts. Encourage children to move beyond the example sentences to other sentences from various texts, such as stories or their own writing. In some cases the subject may not be mentioned in the sentence; for example, games instructions ask the player to *Roll the dice* but do not name the subject. Faced with such examples children would have to infer who does the rolling or leave the space blank.

## Further ideas

● **Look at other passages:** Children can collect cuttings from newspapers and magazines and read through them, circling the various verbs they find. They can look at the tenses of the verbs and determine if a particular tense dominates the text.

● **Tense ping-pong:** As a way of revisiting tenses children can say sentences that describe what they are doing today beginning with the words *Today I....* They can then recreate those sentences in the past tense, beginning *Yesterday I...* This is a good activity to try with a partner. One child begins the activity with a *Today I...* sentence which their partner has to remodel beginning *Yesterday I...*

● **Photographic verbs:** Children can look at pictures of various actions or events in a newspaper and summarise each picture in a sentence. They can then look at the sentence to see if they can locate the verb and the subject.

## What's on the CD-ROM

On the CD-ROM you will find:
● Printable versions of all three photocopiable pages.
● Answers to 'Changing tenses'.
● Interactive version of 'Changing tenses'.

# Verbs

# Odd happenings

■ Look at these extracts from two stories. They present odd scenes and odd happenings. Find some verbs in each passage. Record the action in each verb and who or what is performing the action (the subject).

From *Kasper and the Glitter*
by Philip Ridley

'WOOF!' went a voice.
The dogs stopped in their tracks.
Knucklehead had entered the kitchen.
He was holding the bones that had
been in the pram.
Slowly, Knucklehead went over to the
dogs and said, 'Woof!' once again. This
time in a gentler voice.
The dogs went back to their places by
the oven.
Knucklehead divided the bones
between them, then uttered three
'Woofs' in quick succession and the
dogs started to eat.

| Verb | Subject |
|------|---------|
| went | a voice |
|  |  |
|  |  |
|  |  |
|  |  |
|  |  |
|  |  |
|  |  |
|  |  |
|  |  |

From *The Ghost Drum* by Susan Price

In a place far distant from where you
are now grows an oak-tree by a lake.
Round the oak's trunk is a chain of
golden links.
Tethered to the chain is a learned cat,
and this most learned of all cats walks
round and round the tree continually.
As it walks one way, it sings songs.
As it walks the other, it tells stories.

| Verb | Subject |
|------|---------|
|  |  |
|  |  |
|  |  |
|  |  |
|  |  |
|  |  |
|  |  |
|  |  |

Kasper and the Glitter text © 1994, Philip Ridley; The Ghost Drum text © 1990, Susan Price.

Name:

## Verbs

# Changing tenses

■ Look at these sentences written in the present tense. Change them to the past tense.

| Present tense | Past tense |
|---|---|
| I run and kick the ball. | |
| You sing and we ask you to stop. | |
| He wears scruffy shoes and trips over the laces. | |
| I pour the juice and drink it slowly. | |
| We make a den, paint a sign and hang it on the door. | |
| My aunty climbs the ladder and clears the gutter. | |
| My dad cooks pancakes and tosses them in the air. | |
| The pilot flies the plane and lands it at the airport. | |

# Verbs

# Verb table

■ This table asks for some information about verbs. Use these example sentences to fill in the first few rows.

> Moira threw the ball and broke the window.

> The driver stops the bus and the people get off it.

■ Find some other sentences and use the table to figure things out about the verbs.

| Subject<br>Who is doing the action or to whom is the action happening? | Verb<br>What is the action or happening? | Tense<br>Is it happening in the past, present or future? |
|---|---|---|
| | | |
| | | |
| | | |
| | | |
| | | |
| | | |
| | | |
| | | |
| | | |

# Auxiliary verbs

## Objective

Understand the term 'auxiliary verb'.

## Background knowledge

● **Auxiliary verbs:** are sometimes called 'helping' verbs. They act as auxiliaries to other verbs. They can make the main verb in a phrase conditional. For example, a sentence like *I play Ludo* describes an action I actually do. An auxiliary verb like 'can' slots into the sentence to make *I can play Ludo*. This sentence says that I *can* play it (I am able to), not that I necessarily *do*.

● **Primary verbs:** ('be', 'have', and 'do') can be main verbs: *I am cold. I have a cold. I did nothing.* or auxiliary verbs: *I was making a cake. I have told you once. I didn't see you.*

'Used to', 'ought', 'need' and 'dare' can be used as verbs on their own or as auxiliaries – for example, *I need a drink* or *I need to drink a drink*.

The other auxiliary verbs, the modal verbs, are 'can', 'could', 'may', 'might', 'must', 'will', 'shall', 'would' and 'should'. They always act as auxiliaries to other verbs, such as *I can run*. Auxiliaries can take the 'n't' contraction to form 'haven't', 'wasn't' and 'can't'.

## Activities

Auxiliaries act in support of main verbs. As children encounter auxiliaries this difference needs to be borne in mind. The emphasis in these activities is upon perceiving the difference between main and auxiliary verbs.

● **Photocopiable page 17 'Find the auxiliary'**
By picking apart the quotes from speech, children locate the various auxiliaries. The activity supports the task of differentiating between main verbs and auxiliaries.

● **Photocopiable page 18 'Insert an auxiliary'**
The sentences in this activity can be modified by particular auxiliaries. The children can use the full set of strips and auxiliaries and try swapping them around until they complete all the sentences.

● **Photocopiable page 19 "Don't"**
By reading Michael Rosen's play on the auxiliary verb 'don't', children can be encouraged to find their own examples of auxiliaries with which they can play. Once they have chosen their auxiliary verb or verb phrase encourage them to think of real examples where the verb is used and create ridiculous examples.

## Further ideas

● **Listing:** Before showing children the range of auxiliary verbs they can try to figure out the list for themselves, attempting to list all the auxiliary verbs they know, with examples of sentences using them.

● **Auxiliary setting:** Children can write sentences using auxiliary verbs on slips of paper and present them to a partner who has to decide which is the main verb and which are the auxiliaries.

● **Listen:** Listening to the conversation of adults, children can try locating examples of auxiliary verbs in use. This could extend to a challenge to decide which auxiliary verb is the most commonly used.

## What's on the CD-ROM

On the CD-ROM you will find:
● Printable versions of all three photocopiable pages.
● Answers to 'Find the auxiliary' and 'Insert an auxiliary'.
● Interactive versions of 'Find the auxiliary' and 'Insert an auxiliary'.

## Auxiliary verbs

# Find the auxiliary

■ Look at the speech bubbles below. Find the auxiliary verbs. Circle the main verbs in one colour, and the auxiliary verbs in a different colour.

It won't work!

You don't own the park!

I was told a good joke today.

I am writing a story.

I didn't think it would snow.

The rain has stopped.

I can swim, can't I?

You must change your socks.

We are going to play basketball and you can join us.

Have you heard this joke?

Sam will open the window.

I can see where you hid the key.

The tap is leaking but Mum can fix it.

We must run to the cinema because the film has started.

I might leave my pudding.

I didn't know you were hiding in the basket.

I am so happy I could sing.

I may cook some pancakes – then again I might not.

Josh isn't coming to the party.

Name:

## Auxiliary verbs

# Insert an auxiliary

- The sentences below need verbs to finish them.
- Complete the sentences using the verbs from the bottom of the page.

I _____ painting the wall.

I _____ caught a cold.

I _____ got any money left in my money box.

Our teachers _____ playing football.

My mum _____ going to work.

Please _____ run on the stairs.

If it's sunny we _____ play outside.

My friend _____ run very fast.

After play we _____ go to the classroom.

My mum says I _____ stay away from the railway track.

On Saturday it _____ rain.

My uncle _____ bought a motorbike.

| am | are | is | have | has | haven't |
|----|-----|-----|------|-----|---------|
| don't | can | could | will | should | could |

**PHOTOCOPIABLE**

**SCHOLASTIC**
www.scholastic.co.uk

## Auxiliary verbs

# 'Don't'

■ Read the poem. It plays with the auxiliary verb 'don't'.

■ Could you make up a poem playing with a different auxiliary?

■ It could be a list of things you could do (for example, 'I could eat a horse', 'I could become an astronaut'). It could be as daft as you want. It could be things you will do. It could be things you would like to do. It could be things you wouldn't like to do.

■ Choose an auxiliary verb and play with some of the strange and unusual sentences it conjures up.

**Don't**
Don't do,
Don't do,
Don't do that.
Don't pull faces,
Don't tease the cat.

Don't pick your ears,
Don't be rude at school.
Who do they think I am?

Some kind of fool?

One day
they'll say
Don't put toffee in my coffee
don't pour gravy on the baby
don't put beer in his ear
don't stick your toes up his nose.

Don't put confetti on the spaghetti
and don't squash peas on your knees.

Don't put ants in your pants
don't put mustard in the custard

don't chuck jelly at the telly

and don't throw fruit at the computer
don't throw fruit at the computer.

Don't what?
Don't throw fruit at the computer.
Don't what?
Don't throw fruit at the computer.
What do they think I am?
Some kind of fool?

*Michael Rosen*

*Text © 1985, Michael Rosen; Illustrations © 2008, Moreno Chiacchiera/Beehive Illustration.*

# Verb forms

Examine the forms of verbs in different types of sentence.

## Background knowledge

There are four basic types of sentence:

● **Declarative sentences:** make a statement – for example, *The car is slow*.

● **Interrogative sentences:** ask a question or are phrased in a questioning way – *Is the car slow?* or *The car is slow?*

● **Imperative sentences:** issue commands and orders – *Slow down!*

● **Exclamatory sentences:** make an exclamation and express the emotion of the speaker in the form of an outburst – *Wow, that's slow!*

These four different forms of sentence are called 'moods' in linguistics; there is, therefore, an 'imperative mood', 'interrogative mood' and so on.

## Activities

As children work on these different types of sentence they will notice certain features about the way the verbs change in the different moods.

● **Photocopiable page 21 'Sentence types'**
In looking at the different types of sentence children may notice the way auxiliaries appear in a number of the interrogative sentences and the way the verb is positioned in the imperative.

● **Photocopiable page 22 'Making different forms of sentence'**
Using the verbs and nouns available in the tables, children make sentences in different moods. They can make them as absurd as they wish.

● **Photocopiable page 23 'Verb forms'**
This activity specifically follows the changes in the verbs through sentences that deal with similar subject matter. When children make up their own sentences, they should try to keep the same content but change the mood, noticing the ways in which the verbs change.

## Further ideas

● **Use of mood:** Children can look for different types of sentence around them and see which are most common in certain contexts, such as comics, street signs and so on. When they find an example of a certain type of sentence they can try remodelling the content into a different mood.

## What's on the CD-ROM

On the CD-ROM you will find:
● Printable versions of all three photocopiable pages.
● Answers to 'Sentence types' and 'Verb forms'.
● Interactive version of 'Sentence types'.

# Verb forms

# Sentence types

There are four types of sentence:

| Declarative | Interrogative | Imperative | Exclamatory |
|---|---|---|---|
| States something. | Asks something. | Gives an order. | Exclaims! Sounds surprised! An outburst! |
| The car is slow. | Is the car slow? | Slow down! | Wow, that's slow! |

■ Sort these sentences into **four** groups by type of sentence.

■ To make it more difficult all question marks, exclamation marks and full stops have been removed!

| | | | |
|---|---|---|---|
| When are we having dinner | Go away and leave me alone | Shut up | Hooray |
| School dinners are brilliant | The car isn't working | Brilliant | Walk in a straight line |
| I am going home | What day is it | Get off our train | How long is the table |
| It's Tuesday | Don't tell anyone about our secret | Where did you leave your socks | You are a bit smelly |
| Playtime is cancelled today | I've arrived | Stand still | What a smell |

Name:

# Verb forms

# Making different forms of sentence

■ Using the verbs and nouns in the tables below, can you make the types of sentence asked for?

You can change the verb from one form to another. Instead of using 'make', you could change it to 'made'.

| Verb: make | Nouns: sandwich, string | Sentence type: declarative |
|---|---|---|
| | | |

| Verb: find | Nouns: shoes, table | Sentence type: declarative |
|---|---|---|
| | | |

| Verb: eat | Nouns: custard, cabbage | Sentence type: interrogative |
|---|---|---|
| | | |

| Verb: sniff | Nouns: dog, classroom | Sentence type: interrogative |
|---|---|---|
| | | |

| Verb: tell | Nouns: lemons, home | Sentence type: declarative |
|---|---|---|
| | | |

| Verb: shout | Nouns: street, sock | Sentence type: imperative |
|---|---|---|
| | | |

Illustrations © 2008, Moreno Chiacchiera/Beehive Illustration.

**PHOTOCOPIABLE**

# Verb forms

# Verb forms

■ Look at this table. It shows a verb in its simple form. Can you change the verb so that it fits into the space in each of the sentences?

| Simple verb | Declarative | Interrogative | Imperative |
|---|---|---|---|
| to find | We _____ the lost key. | Can you _____ the lost key? | _____ the lost key. |
| to tell | Our teacher _____ good jokes. | Does our teacher _____ good jokes? | _____ us a joke. |
| to eat | Every morning my mum _____ toast for breakfast. | What did your mum _____ for breakfast? | _____ your breakfast. |
| to go | The car _____ down the street. | Where does the car _____? | _____ down the street. |

■ Now choose **two** of your own verbs. Write sentences for each, changing the verb to fit the different types of sentence.

Declarative

_____

Interrogative

_____

Imperative

_____

Declarative

_____

Interrogative

_____

Imperative

_____

**■SCHOLASTIC**
www.scholastic.co.uk     **PHOTOCOPIABLE**                              **Scholastic Literacy Skills**
Grammar and punctuation: Year 5   **23**

# Person

## Objective

Identify and experiment with person in verbs.

## Background knowledge

Verbs are linked to subjects. A subject is the 'who' or 'what' behind a verb. In *I swam*, the subject is 'I' and the verb is 'swam'. If a command is issued, such as *Jump* the verb is 'jump' and the subject is whoever the command is addressed to. Subjects and verbs can be in the first, second or third person. The different types of person are indicated by the use of subject pronouns (for example, 'I', 'she') and verbs.

● **First-person verbs:** identify with the speaker or writer, either alone (*I swam*) or as part of a group (*we swam*).

● **Second-person verbs:** identify with one addressed by the speaking or writing (*You must remember…*).

● **Third-person verbs:** identify with a third party or thing who is neither the one addressing nor the one addressed (*He shouted*; *It fell*).

## Activities

An understanding of person is essential as children develop the range of writing they produce. Certain texts, such as instructions or postcards, will address the reader directly in the second person (*First you take an egg…*, *Wish you were here…*), whereas other texts will favour other uses of person, such as diaries in the first person or reports of events in the third person.

● **Photocopiable page 25 'Person switching'**
As they switch sentences from one person to another children can look for the different words that change and those that stay the same. When putting a sentence into the third person it is up to them which gender form they use.

● **Photocopiable page 26 'Correct the sentences'**
Children work through these postcards, editing the writing of the Language Bug until it sounds right. Once they have worked on these examples they may want to send examples to one another.

● **Photocopiable page 27 'The rabbit's poem'**
This is a classic nonsense poem that plays with different persons. Once children have tried to locate the three forms of person requested in the activity, they could look for other verbal material, such as the use of the auxiliary verb or the use of singular or plural persons.

## Further ideas

● **Who is 'she'?:** Children can look at a text and find the various subject pronouns. They then have to write the type of pronoun identified by these words in the margin or in the space above them.

● **How would the text change?:** Looking at various texts, ask children to work in pairs re-reading them but changing the person. If they are reading a first-person text they can put it into second or third person.

● **Debate:** Look at texts that use a third-person form for general reference. Find examples and discuss them with the class. Do they think it is the right way to make general references? Can they think of an alternative?

## What's on the CD-ROM

On the CD-ROM you will find:
● Printable versions of all three photocopiable pages.
● Answers to all three photocopiable pages.
● Interactive version of 'Correct the sentences'.

## Person

# Person switching

Verbs can be written in the first person, second person or third person.

| First-person verbs | refer to the writer. |
|---|---|
| Second-person verbs | refer to the reader. |
| Third-person verbs | refer to other things or people. |

■ Rewrite the sentences in the spaces below.
- Change any sentences written in the first person to the second person.
- Change any sentences written in the second person to the third person.
- Change any sentences written in the third person to the first person.

■ Which verbs changed and which stayed the same? Which other words changed?

I am going to school. _____

You play the piano. _____

He shouts his name. _____

I support United. _____

You draw brilliant pictures. _____

She says the alphabet quickly. _____

You were singing. _____

He climbed the rope. _____

They play in the park. _____

I am all on my own. _____

Name:

## Person

# Correct the sentences

■ Look at the sentences in these letters. Mark the changes that need to be made so that the sentences read correctly. The first one has been done for you.

change

Dear You
Can you (changing) the verbs on
this letter so it sound right?
Once you has finished reads it
back to checking your changes.
Remember verbs need to agrees
with the rest of the sentence so
you is going to have to changes
them.
Yours, The Language Bug!

Dear You
You was very clever. I were sure
you will not be able to change my
last card but you do. Anyway,
this one am much harder so see
if you makes the right changes
this time. Takes care, there is
lots of little traps tucks into the
sentences.

Yours, The Language Bug!

Dear You
Curses you be too clever for
me. I gives up. It annoy me
that you is so good at spot
my handiwork. But I will
being back another day and
will teaches you a lesson.
Next time I am win. Me will
triumph! Until then sits back
and relax because these is
my last mistakes. Or is they?
Yours, The Language Bug!

Illustrations © 2008, Moreno Chiacchiera/Beehive Illustration.

**PHOTOCOPIABLE**

■SCHOLASTIC
www.scholastic.co.uk

## Person

# The rabbit's poem

■ Look at this classic poem and circle or shade over three different types of verb and subject pronoun in three different colours:

- First-person verbs and pronouns in green.
- Second-person verbs and pronouns in blue.
- Third-person verbs and pronouns in red.

**The rabbit's poem**

'They told me you had been to her,
And mentioned me to him:
She gave me a good character,
But said I could not swim.

He sent them word I had not gone
(We know it to be true):
If she should push the matter on,
What would become of you?

I gave her one, they gave him two,
You have us three or more;
They all returned from him to you,
Though they were mine before.

If I or she should chance to be
Involved in this affair,
He trusts to you to set them free,
Exactly as we were.

My notion was that you had been
(Before she had this fit)
An obstacle that came between
Him, and ourselves, and it.

Don't let him know she liked them best,
For this must ever be
A secret, kept from all the rest,
Between yourself and me.'

*Lewis Carroll*

# Verbs in writing

## Objective

Develop the use of verbs in writing.

## Writing focus

These activities take various features of verbs, such as the future tense and the modal verb, and explore some of the potential these offer for creative writing.

## Skills to writing

### ● Tense switching

Switch sentences between tenses. During shared or guided writing, as children are devising various sentences, ask them to consider what it would be like if it were written in a different tense. No need to write these – but they are worth sharing quickly and verbally.

### ● Conversations

Taking the various types of sentence, look at conversations in longer stories and novels, seeking out examples where different sentence types have been used. The use of question and answer is a particularly useful focus for children, with a view towards developing their writing. At this stage in their writing children should be encouraged to write more extensive conversations in their narratives, particularly ones in which characters unpick their impressions of events that are taking place and answer conflicts or tensions in the story. An exchange with question and answer can provide a great vehicle for this sort of conversation within a story.

### ● Emotions

Watch out for the emotional mood in a sentence – particularly in speech. If someone says *I'm sorry!* or *Look out*, how were they feeling? Taking a range of texts from a tabloid paper it's possible to find a range of emotions coming through the editorial, opinion, television critique, sports opinion and letters pages. Encourage the children to find the ways in which different sentences make it clear how the writer was feeling.

### ● Modal meaning

Examine the varying ways in which modal verbs affect the action presented in a sentence. This is a feature of conversation – and one quite common in schools. When the children ask the Head *Will we all be going to the pantomime this year?* the answer *We will* is very different from *We could* or *We might*. It also avoids having to say *We won't*. Tune children in to 'spot the modal' – whether in conversation at school or examples shared from home (*Mum, can I go to town with my friends? You might be able to*). As they catch various examples, encourage them to look out for how certain or fudged the action is, when the modal is used. (I recall the time a girl said, in school council, responding to my *We may…* with the words, *Is that a 'yes' or a 'no'?*)

### ● Persuasive modals

Watch out for the use of the modal in persuasive writing. The firm declaration that something will lead to a result is different from the threat that it might. The notion that children watching soap operas might result in them becoming rude, or the leaflet suggesting that a new road could increase traffic through a village, are the sorts of modal usages that can raise spectres for persuasive purposes.

## Activities

### ● Photocopiable page 30 'I might…'

The photocopiable sheet presents a range of options for the use of modal verbs in conversation. Children can use this to make notes as part of the process of narrative writing. To do this, they need to select a scenario, then in each of the speech bubbles they need to write something a characters could say at this point in the story. Can they use these lines in their story writing?

### ● Photocopiable page 31 'Movement verbs'

This activity introduces children to a set of verbs that can be used to denote movement – a useful resource when writing narrative. Children should use the spaces alongside the verbs to make notes – either of the sort of sentence they think could contain such a verb, asking questions like *When would someone lunge?* or making short notes about the type of movement they think is denoted by the verb. *Is it fast or slow? What sort of direction does it take?*

## Write on

● **Rabbit's lines**

Children can use photocopiable page 27 'Rabbit's poem' as a model for their own poem, in which a complicated exchange between various characters is wrapped up in sentences that depict all the events in pronoun. Don't worry about rhyme, the children should aim to make mysterious sentences – but the key is if the author is then asked to explain what it's all about they should be able to, and readers should be able to follow the various 'he' and 'she' characters as they engage with 'it'.

● **Write a future**

Exercise the future tense by asking children to write their dream future. Tell them the four rules for this to work well are that they must dream big dreams, the best they can imagine; they must also write about more than just their job (so we don't just get 500 words on playing for Manchester United); they must imagine a career change in there somewhere and they must try to include some features that no one else in the room has thought or dreamed of. As they write this, ask them to vary the level of certainty, moving between what they 'will', 'might' and 'could do'.

● **Isaiah 53**

In this Old Testament poem the people of Israel and/ or Jesus are spoken of as being like a Suffering Servant who endured various trials. Whether the children fully understand it or not, the poem makes for a text that can be read aloud and allowed to project its mystery. Who is he, she and they in this poem? What happens to him?

● **Don't poems**

Children spend much of their days faced with rules. Can they list some of the best and turn these into a list poem similar to the Michael Rosen example on photocopiable page 19? The secret of this poem is that it starts with ones we would normally encounter and then mixes them and changes words, until the resultant list of imperatives is absurd. Can the children take theirs in a similar direction?

● **Product rules**

Ask the children to look at warnings on products to see if they can come up with some examples of strange do and don't instructions. Some of the best examples are collected in books like *Wearing of this Garment Does Not Enable You to Fly: And Other Really Dumb Warnings*, by Jeff Koon and Andy Powell (Simon & Schuster), including the warning on a baby lotion that reads: Keep away from children.

### What's on the CD-ROM

On the CD-ROM you will find:
● Printable versions of both photocopiable pages.

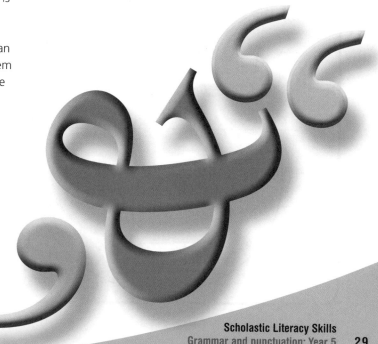

Name:

# Verbs in writing

# I might...

■ Use these sentence starters to plan the things your characters might, could or should say.

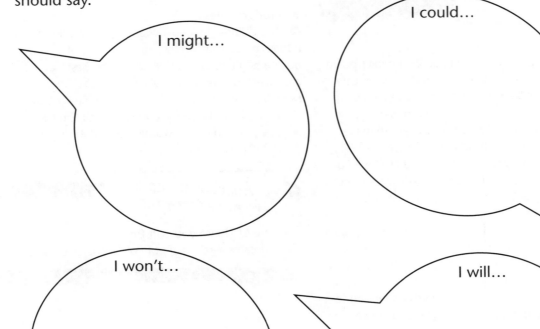

I might...

I could...

I won't...

I will...

I should...

I mustn't...

## Verbs in writing

# Movement verbs

■ How could you use these movement verbs? Plan some sentences you could write with them, in the spaces below.

| | |
|---|---|
| lunged | |
| plummeted | |
| dived | |
| hurtled | |
| skidded | |
| pursued | |
| tottered | |
| teetered | |

# Pronouns and nouns

## Introduction

This chapter focuses upon pronouns. The main elements of this focus are a look at the way in which pronouns stand in for nouns, and the effects this can have on the clarity of a sentence.

## Poster notes

### Types of nouns (page 33)
This poster provides a brief summation of the qualities of a noun and supports the revision activities in 'Noun sorts'. As children investigate the function of nouns the poster provides a way of identifying them within sentences.

### Pronouns (page 34)
The poster links with 'The function of pronouns' and provides a reference point showing the various types of pronoun. As children work on pronouns it provides a useful resource to refer to, defining the different jobs that pronouns can do. The classification of pronouns is a complex activity but this poster can provide an insight into the wide range of words that are included in this word class.

## In this chapter

| Noun sorts page 35 | Revisit the different types of noun. |
| --- | --- |
| The function of pronouns page 39 | Revise the function of pronouns. |
| Noun and pronoun play page 43 | Investigate the function of pronouns and their reference. |
| Apostrophe of possession page 47 | Revise the use of the apostrophe for possession. |
| Nouns, pronouns and writing page 51 | Develop the use of nouns and pronouns in writing. |

**Pronouns and nouns**

# Types of nouns

A noun is a word for a thing.

It could be a thing you feel.

It could be a thing you see.

It could be an abstract thing you just know.

*happiness*

*heat*

*dog*

If you can imagine saying 'a', 'an' or 'the' before a word – then it is a noun.

*Illustrations © 2008, Moreno Chiacchiera/Beehive Illustration.*

# Pronouns

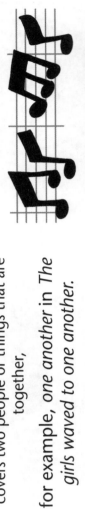

**personal**

indicates a person, for example, *she* in *She plays football.*

**reflexive**

refers to someone or something already mentioned in the sentence, for example, *herself* in *She made tea for herself.*

**relative**

links one part of a sentence to another, for example, *who* in *Joe is a boy who likes singing.*

**reciprocal**

covers two people or things that are together, for example, *one another* in *The girls waved to one another.*

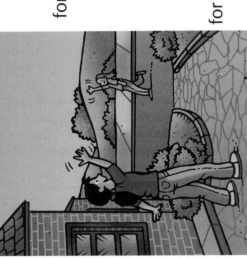

**demonstrative**

points to a particular noun mentioned in the text, for example, *this* in *This is my house.*

**interrogative**

used in questions, for example, *who* in *Who is having tea?*

**indefinite**

refers to someone or something without knowing its name, for example, *something* in *Something made a noise.*

# Noun sorts

## Objective

Revisit the different types of noun.

## Background knowledge

Nouns are words that name things or feelings. This class of words includes all words that can act as subjects in a sentence, so if a word can follow the articles 'a', 'an' or 'the' in a sentence then it is a noun. This means that words like 'walk', which would commonly be classed as a verb, can be classed as a noun in a sentence like *We are going for a walk*. The verb here is 'going', because that is the action 'we' are taking. Nouns can often be detected by the way they can be turned from singular to plural and vice versa. In this example 'We' could go for a number of 'walks': *We are going for a few walks*. Although the plurals made may seem odd, the pluralisation rule acts as another useful test of a noun.

## Activities

The ability to say 'a', 'an' and 'the' before a word, along with the pluralisation test, provide two ways of identifying nouns. In these activities children investigate the process of identifying nouns and revisit some of the different types of nouns.

● **Photocopiable page 36 'Is this a noun?'**
In applying the 'a', 'an' or 'the' test children can be asked to think of a context in which a construction can work. It is difficult to think of an example in which we would say 'a soft' but we can imagine talking about 'a jump' in a context like *She did a brilliant jump*. This helps us to determine which of these two words could be used as a noun.

● **Photocopiable page 37 'Finding nouns'**
As children swap the nouns around in this activity they will need to check that the sentences they make include consistent uses of single and plural nouns.

● **Photocopiable page 38 'Nounsearch'**
As they undertake this activity children will need to be reminded of the various types of nouns (see poster page 33 'Types of nouns').

## Further ideas

● **Headlines:** Look at the headlines of newspaper stories. Ask the children to find words that are used as nouns in the headlines but could be used as verbs in a different sentence, for example, *Talks crumble in Union row*. They can cut them out and create the new sentence around them.
● **Dictionary nouns:** Taking any page in the dictionary, children can go through the words listed testing them to see if they could be used as nouns.
● **Jumble sentences:** Taking several sentences from a story, children can try jumbling the nouns around to make a nonsensical opening.

## What's on the CD-ROM

On the CD-ROM you will find:
● Printable versions of all three photocopiable pages.
● Answers to 'Is this a noun?' and 'Nounsearch'.
● Interactive versions of 'Is this a noun?' and 'Finding nouns'.

Name:

## Noun sorts

# Is this a noun?

If you can imagine saying 'a', 'an' or 'the' before a word – then it is a noun.

A noun is a word for a thing.

It could be a thing you see.

It could be a thing you feel.

It could be an abstract thing you just know. For example: An understanding

■ Sort these words into **two** separate lists:
- words we could use as nouns
- words we don't use as nouns.

| heard | children | can | always | dog |
|-------|----------|------|--------|---------|
| can't | happy | sure | apple | sound |
| flat | until | swim | soft | where |
| jump | light | through | word | stopped |

Illustrations © 2008, Moreno Chiacchiera/Beehive Illustration.

**PHOTOCOPIABLE**

## Noun sorts

# Finding nouns

■ Cut out the nouns from these sentences and swap them round to make new sentences. For example:

| Please pass the sugar |
|---|

and

| Don't feed the tiger |
|---|

| Please pass the | tiger |
|---|---|

Could be cut
and pasted into:

| Don't feed the | sugar |
|---|---|

✂- - - - - - - - - - - - - - - - - - - - - - - - - - - - - - - - - - - - - - - - - - - - - - -

| Please pass the sugar. |
|---|
| The pencils need sharpening. |
| Can I eat a biscuit? |
| Don't feed the tiger. |
| The rain is heavy, use this umbrella. |
| Quick! Pass me the fire extinguisher. |
| Could I borrow your handkerchief? |
| You can throw those sweet wrappers in the bin. |
| We ate fish and chips for tea. |
| I put your dirty socks and pants in the laundry basket. |

Illustrations © 2008, Moreno Chiacchiera/Beehive Illustration.

Name:

## Noun sorts

# Nounsearch

A **concrete noun** is something you can see such as a dog or a book.

An **abstract noun** refers to a noun which is not concrete. It could be an action, an event or a state, such as 'worry' or 'happiness'.

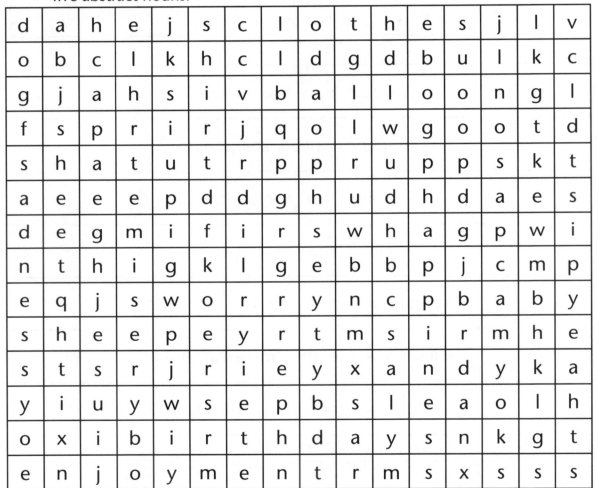

■ Look for the following and shade each type in a different colour

- five singular concrete nouns.
- five plural concrete nouns.
- five abstract nouns.

| d | a | h | e | j | s | c | l | o | t | h | e | s | j | l | v |
|---|---|---|---|---|---|---|---|---|---|---|---|---|---|---|---|
| o | b | c | l | k | h | c | l | d | g | d | b | u | l | k | c |
| g | j | a | h | s | i | v | b | a | l | l | o | o | n | g | l |
| f | s | p | r | i | r | j | q | o | l | w | g | o | o | t | d |
| s | h | a | t | u | t | r | p | p | r | u | p | p | s | k | t |
| a | e | e | e | p | d | d | g | h | u | d | h | d | a | e | s |
| d | e | g | m | i | f | i | r | s | w | h | a | g | p | w | i |
| n | t | h | i | g | k | l | g | e | b | b | p | j | c | m | p |
| e | q | j | s | w | o | r | r | y | n | c | p | b | a | b | y |
| s | h | e | e | p | e | y | r | t | m | s | i | r | m | h | e |
| s | t | s | r | j | r | i | e | y | x | a | n | d | y | k | a |
| y | i | u | y | w | s | e | p | b | s | l | e | a | o | l | h |
| o | x | i | b | i | r | t | h | d | a | y | s | n | k | g | t |
| e | n | j | o | y | m | e | n | t | r | m | s | x | s | s | s |

| dog | books | dogs | sadness | happiness |
|-----|-------|------|---------|-----------|
| balloon | clothes | birthdays | shirt | misery |
| baby | worry | enjoyment | sheet | sheep |

Illustrations © 2008, Moreno Chiacchiera/Beehive Illustration.

# The function of pronouns

## Objective

Revise the function of pronouns.

## Background knowledge

Pronouns are words that act as substitutes for nouns. If, instead of saying, *Jack ate breakfast* we substitute 'it' for the noun 'breakfast' we make the new sentence *Jack ate it*. There are different functions pronouns can perform:
- **Demonstrative:** this is when pronouns point out a specific thing, such as 'this', 'that'.
- **Interrogative:** these are pronouns that raise a question, such as 'which' and 'what'. They refer to the noun that forms the answer to the question. For example, in the question *What is London?* the pronoun 'What' stands in for the noun *A city*.
- **Indefinite:** a pronoun can be used to stand for the person or quantity not yet identified such as 'anyone' or 'something'.
- **Personal:** pronouns that refer to people such as 'she', 'we' and 'they'.
- **Reflexive:** pronouns which end in a form of '-self', such as 'himself' and 'ourselves'.
- **Relative:** linking information about a noun to the noun, such as 'who' in *the man who lives here*, and 'that' in *the dog that dug a hole*.
- **Reciprocal:** used to cover parties relating to one another, such as 'one another'. In the sentence *Jack and Jill blamed one another* the reciprocal pronoun 'one another' stands in for 'Jack and Jill'.

## Activities

The categories of pronoun are complex and the emphasis of these activities is not upon children learning each of them. Instead they encourage children to reflect upon the fact that there are different ways in which pronouns can take the place of nouns.

- **Photocopiable page 40 'Find the pronouns'**
As a revision of pronouns, this activity involves locating them in sentences. One way into this activity is for children to delete words they are sure are *not* pronouns.
- **Photocopiable page 41 'Types of pronouns'**
After looking at the definitions of pronouns, children are asked to locate examples for each one. There are two examples for each definition, but it is up to the teacher whether or not to tell that to the class.
- **Photocopiable page 42 'The door'**
This story plays with pronouns. Children are asked to locate different types of pronoun in the story.

## Further ideas

- **Pop pronouns:** Children can guess which type of pronoun is the most common and then participate in a tallying activity, reading texts and charting how often a particular type of pronoun appears.
- **Extend the examples:** Ask the children to try and find more examples of the different types of pronoun other than those given here.

## What's on the CD-ROM

On the CD-ROM you will find:
- Printable versions of all three photocopiable pages.
- Answers to 'Find the pronouns' and 'Types of pronouns'.
- Interactive version of 'Find the pronouns'.

**The function of pronouns**

# Find the pronouns

■ Find the pronouns in these sentences and circle them.
■ Are they referring to things or people and are they asking questions?

This is my house.

That is the fire escape.

What is the capital city of Egypt?

Where is the light switch?

Does anyone want a cup of tea?

Someone tidied up.

She is playing football.

We are going there after school.

I can cook for myself.

My mum treated herself to this bar of chocolate.

Can you stop arguing with each other?

This is the book that I lost yesterday.

**The function
of pronouns**

# Types of pronouns

There are seven different types of pronoun – demonstrative, interrogative, indefinite, personal, reflexive, relative and reciprocal.

■   For each sentence circle the pronoun and identify the pronoun type.

| | |
|---|---|
| These are my hands. | |
| What is your name? | |
| Which coat is yours? | |
| Yuck – something smells bad! | |
| They are eating cakes. | |
| That was a good game. | |
| Share your ideas with one another. | |
| The boy hurt himself on the climbing frame. | |
| We are hungry. | |
| Sam is the boy whose mum flies aeroplanes. | |
| The children helped each other make dinner. | |
| Somebody made a mess. | |
| You can help yourself to sandwiches. | |
| Mavis is a goat who can sing. | |

Name:

# The door

■ Look at the text below. Find the pronouns and circle them. Underline each type of pronoun in a different colour.

### The story with a creepy house

They approached the house that stood, deserted, beyond the trees. They were all scared but she persuaded them to walk right up to that open door she had seen from the road. She pushed the door open.

"Where are you going?" somebody asked.

"I have come this far," she replied "I am not going back."

Someone said "We won't go in there."

"Suit yourself," she said, too late.

They had run away.

She stepped inside, reassuring herself by saying aloud, "I don't need them. I can look after myself," as slowly, the door creaked shut behind her.

# Noun and pronoun play

## Objective

Investigate the function of pronouns and their reference.

## Background knowledge

Pronouns can be odd words to use. They are confusing without a clear idea of who or what they are referring to. This is a feature that can be used to full effect in advertising slogans such as *You know it makes sense*. The slogan is memorable but vague enough to make us wonder what the pithy little sentence referred to. The vagueness and ambiguity of pronouns are also at the root of humorous exchanges such as the style of joke used many times in the film *Airplane*:

● Passenger: Hostess, take me to the cockpit!
● Hostess:     What is it?
● Passenger: It's a little room at the front of the plane with controls and things, but that's not important right now.

## Activities

These activities allow a bit of enjoyment of the ambiguity of pronouns. The examples included show various levels of playing with pronouns and trying to decipher what they refer to.

● **Photocopiable page 44 'Knots'**
If children take an interest in *Knots* by RD Laing (Penguin Books) in this activity it may be worth showing them some others selected from the book. Some are very complex but there are a few innovative and entertaining ones that children can enjoy.

● **Photocopiable page 45 'Who is who?'**
As they explore the reference of various pronouns children will find some interesting examples in this passage. There are pronouns that refer to the reader and pronouns that denote the narrator ('I...'). One subject this passage raises for discussion is how we know certain people are referred to by the specific pronouns.

● **Photocopiable page 46 'Two ways of reading it'**
The ambiguity of pronouns can result in some interesting sentences. In these examples there are two ways of reading each sentence and, while there may be an obvious reading, it is tempting to explore the alternative.

## Further ideas

● **Retell stories:** Children can try retelling well known stories as pronoun tales, seeing how reductive their result can be and if anyone can recognise the original story from the end result. For example:
*They went out. She came in. Didn't eat his. Didn't eat hers but did eat his. Didn't sit on his, didn't sit on hers but did sit on his.*
Do you recognise *Goldilocks and the Three Bears*?

● **Something Else:** *Something Else* by Kathryn Cave (Picture Puffins) is a picture book in which the characters' names are made up of pronouns. It proves to be an excellent story about how an 'I' accepts a 'You', making a 'They' friendship.

● **Script pointing:** Look in other scripts to see how items and people in the text are referred to using pronouns and how this may lead the actor to point or use other gestures to indicate who is being referred to.

## What's on the CD-ROM

On the CD-ROM you will find:
● Printable versions of all three photocopiable pages.
● Answers to 'Two ways of reading it'.
● Interactive version of 'Two ways of reading it'.

Name:

# Knots

In 1969 RD Laing published a book of poems about the way people relate to other people and things. He called the poems *Knots*. Here are two of them.

■ Look at the poems. What do you think they are about? How do they cleverly use pronouns? Could you write a poem using pronouns in a similar way?

> They are playing a game. They are playing at not
> playing a game. If I show them I see they are, I
> shall break the rules and they will punish me.
> I must play their game, of not seeing I see the game.

*RD Laing*

I want it
I get it
therefore I am good

I want it
I don't get it
therefore I am bad

I am bad
    because I didn't get it

I am bad
    because I wanted what I didn't get

I must take care
    to get what I want
    and want what I get
    and not get what I don't want

*RD Laing*

Text © 1970, RD Laing; Illustrations © 2008, Moreno Chiacchiera/Beehive Illustration.

**Noun and pronoun play**

# Who is who?

■ Circle the pronouns in this passage from Andrew Gibson's 'The Great Querne' (from the book *The Rollickers*). Can you point out who or what each pronoun refers to?

There were four of them: Thornton, Ern, Roxella and the Duchess. They were all children; all of them were unusual; and I shall not try to tell you how they got their names – or rather, if I remember rightly, nicknames. They were all sitting in a small room, hugging their knees, and looking very miserable.

'I had not realised,' said the Duchess, pulling thoughtfully at one of her many red curls, 'that life could be so flat'.

'Nor me, Duchess' said Thornton, 'nor me'.

Thornton and the Duchess spoke in a rather peculiar way, and you may as well get used to it now.

'Whose fault is it, Thornton?' the Duchess asked. She had something of a soft spot for him, …

Name:

**Noun and pronoun play**

# Two ways of reading it

■ Look at these sentences. Each of them could be read in two ways. In the first one the pronoun 'He' could refer to the dog – or Harry! Try finding the possible double meanings for each of the other sentences.

My friend Harry has got a dog. He is smelly.

Harry smells. | The dog smells.

Our school had a bike shed but it got knocked down.

The teachers played football against the children and they lost.

My brother and sister found some broken toys so we put them in the bin.

Our teacher has got a gerbil. We like watching him run round in his wheel.

I looked in the car for my glove but found it in the washing machine.

My sisters fed the rabbits. They have floppy ears and funny teeth.

# Apostrophe of possession

## Objective

Revise the use of the apostrophe for possession.

## Background knowledge

Apostrophes can be used to show possession. An apostrophe on a noun shows that it possesses a following item – for example *Sean's book*. Rules for adding apostrophes depend upon the noun to which it is being added.

● **If the noun is singular and doesn't end in 's':** you add an apostrophe and an 's' for example, *Sam's dog.*

● **If the noun is singular and ends in 's':** you add an apostrophe and an 's' for example, *Ross's dog. Paris's tower.*

● **If the noun is plural and doesn't end in 's':** you add an apostrophe and an 's' for example, *The children's dog. The mice's nest.*

● **If the noun is plural and ends in 's':** you add an apostrophe but *don't* add an 's' for example, *The babies' rattles. The teachers' mugs.*

## Activities

These activities present a brief review of the use of the apostrophe. Emphasis is placed upon the way in which it is added to a noun to show possession.

● **Photocopiable page 48 'Noun grid'**
The grid looks at the way nouns are classified when apostrophes are being added. Children cut out the nouns shown and sort them on to the Carroll diagram, matching the column and row to place nouns correctly. By placing nouns on the grid, children are making the sort of classification they will use when they add apostrophes.

● **Photocopiable page 49 'Placing apostrophes'**
This activity presents a review of the rules for using the apostrophe. Children then use these in placing apostrophes in the sentences shown.

● **Photocopiable page 50 'Apostrophes in sentences'**
As they use the nouns shown in a possessive form in sentences, children will need to consider how the noun endings take the apostrophe.

## Further ideas

● **Apostrophe use:** Children can look at their own use of the apostrophe in recent work, possibly using the 'Noun grid' to analyse words they have used. They can check the correctness of their placing of the apostrophe.

## What's on the CD-ROM

On the CD-ROM you will find:
● Printable versions of all three photocopiable pages.
● Answers to 'Noun grid' and 'Placing apostrophes'.
● Interactive versions of 'Noun grid' and 'Placing apostrophes'.

Name:

**Apostrophe of possession**

# Noun grid

■ Cut out the words at the bottom of the page and sort them into the Carroll diagram below.

|  | **Does not end in 's'** | **Ends in 's'** |
|---|---|---|
| **Singular** |  |  |
| **Plural** |  |  |

✂ ----

| Kate | Ross | Mr Harris | woman | geese | Paris | mice |
|---|---|---|---|---|---|---|
| fishes | women | dogs | coats | Sam | children | dog |

**Apostrophe of possession**

# Placing apostrophes

Here are the rules for the use of apostrophes.

| | |
|---|---|
| If the noun is singular and doesn't end in 's' you add an apostrophe and an 's', for example: Sam's dog. | If the noun is singular and ends in 's' you add an apostrophe and an 's', for example: Ross's dog Paris's tower. |
| If the noun is plural and doesn't end in 's' you add an apostrophe and an 's', for example: the children's dog the mice's nest. | If the noun is plural and ends in 's' you add an apostrophe but *don't* add an 's', for example: the babies' rattles the teachers' mugs. |

■ Rewrite these sentences using apostrophes.

The fishes water was cleaned. _____

We mended Grans window. _____

Mr Thomass classroom is untidy. _____

Liams mum is a doctor. _____

My schools playtime is in the morning. _____

The womens meeting is postponed. _____

The thieves plans were devious. _____

My classs assembly is on Tuesday. _____

I flew Ryans kite. _____

This shop sells mens clothes. _____

The childrens teacher ran away. _____

Name:

# Apostrophes in sentences

■ Look at this list of owners.

| princess | dragons | leopard | bookseller |
|----------|---------|---------|------------|
| teacher | children | babies | cook |
| cows | hippopotamuses | firefighter | Prime Minister |

■ Think of an item each of them could own. Write a sentence about them and the item that they own. Use an apostrophe to show that they own the item.

_____

_____

_____

_____

_____

_____

_____

_____

_____

# Nouns, pronouns and writing

## Objective

Develop the use of nouns and pronouns in writing.

## Writing focus

In these activities, children's use of nouns and pronouns is expanded into various bits of writing play that will get them experimenting with this word class.

## Skills to writing

### ● Noun planning

Nouns support planning. When thinking ahead to a report text, children can structure their writing by thinking of the nouns related to their subject. Children who haven't made a start on writing about a subject, will often suddenly gain ideas when asked to list a set of nouns associated with a subject.

### ● Abstract nouns

Abstract nouns can be a great tool for all sorts of writing stimulus. Words like 'happiness' and 'fear' conjure up interesting material for a different sort of report text. While reports tend to be written about concrete subjects, an abstract noun can provide an interesting stimulus that results in more diverse writing. If children are asked to write about anger, the subject matter is there at hand, looking at what makes people angry, what happens when they are angry and how this can be handled. A chance to get it out of their system.

### ● What's the abstract?

Abstract nouns also provide an excellent resource for developing the sort of group talk that can enhance children's writing. When faced with a subject like 'hope' children can express their own hopes for the future. However, for their writing to be really effective, encourage them to listen to the thoughts and experiences of others with a view towards drawing these into their text. When thinking about 'worries', listening to the experiences of others might help children to start seeing some common factors encountered in this abstract concept – such as, worries being alleviated when they're talked through.

### ● Scary pronoun

Pronouns provide some great opportunities for creating mystery in texts. Look out for examples in scary stories (She opened the door. That was when she saw *it* for the first time). Draw children's attention to the way their use raises questions that hook the reader.

### ● The subject

Maintain a regular habit of stopping at a pronoun and reflecting on the subject. One interesting resource here is newspaper headlines, where a sentence like *It's over!* assumes a knowledge of the story. Even the famous *Sun* headline *Gotcha* carried an implicit second person 'cha'. When this occurs, readers need to figure out the subject.

### ● Word origins

Origins of nouns can be particularly interesting. There are words like 'sandwich', named after a person, but other nouns have equally interesting origins worth researching. Libraries and the internet can provide sources for exploring the cricketing origins of the 'hat-trick' – which was originally a hat given by a club to a bowler who had bowled three batsmen. And 'quiz' – a totally invented noun. Nouns are names, and often there is a history behind the name.

## Activities

### ● Photocopiable page 53 'Abstract thinking'

This photocopiable sheet is designed to stimulate children's thinking about abstract nouns. Children list their initial thoughts and responses to the abstract nouns presented. When they encounter these words, what do they think of? Are there particular experiences they would jot down? Are there people they associate with, for example, a feeling like happiness?

### ● Photocopiable page 54 'She did what?'

Before cutting up the grid, look across the columns and find the potential for stories. *He found it*, is different to *He found her*. To work with this activity, children need to cut out the words on the photocopiable sheet and arrange them on the table. Working in twos they shuffle the words around, looking at some of the mini-stories or story events they create by putting three words together, such as *I saw it*, and then asking questions such as: *What might I have seen? Why was it so important?* Children make a mini-story, discuss it and note down any good ideas it generates.

## Write on

### ● Write a knot

Children can use photocopiable page 44 'Knots' as a stimulus for writing. The idea is to write a short, interpersonal dilemma using pronouns over a few lines. These can be kept simple and record a common experience. For example:

*I want to.*
*You don't.*
*We argue.*
*We don't.*

Once finished children can share their writing with each other and may find other thoughts inform their writing and new lines creep in. For example, adding *You didn't want to argue*, at the end of the earlier example.

### ● Ambiguous pronouns

Children can play with ambiguous pronouns in their writing. Lines like *The boy ran up to the dog. He bit him*, leave us wondering who bit who. Children could try using this idea in a short piece of writing. The basic idea is to script a conversation between two people where the use of a pronoun causes confusion. Someone says something clear and then uses pronouns. For example: *The boy ran up to the dog, and he bit him* and a listener responds with the confusion: *The boy bit the dog?* This isn't easy, but children like the idea.

### ● Abstract stories

Abstract nouns can provide stimulus for either devising stories or collecting real reminiscences. Given one like 'worry', children can reflect on what it's like to feel worried, lose sleep over a worry, and face up to the worry. Such thinking can provide the makings of a good story. Jacqueline Wilson's novels expertly capture some of the abstract feelings of childhood such as envy, worry and happiness.

### ● Creepy door

Children can both write and record their own creepy texts similar to photocopiable page 42 'The door' and then record these. Sustain the mystery through the ambiguous language – mystery pronouns really help. *He looked up the staircase. Was she up there?* As the children produce an audio version, they need to ask how they will modulate the voice of the teller and what sound effects they could add.

## What's on the CD-ROM

On the CD-ROM you will find:
● Printable versions of both photocopiable pages.

**Nouns, pronouns and writing**

# Abstract thinking

■ Look at the words below. What thoughts and ideas do they conjure up? Jot some of these in the spaces alongside each word.

| | |
|---|---|
| happiness | worry |
| envy | hate |
| difficulty | peace |
| thoughtfulness | anger |

**SCHOLASTIC**
www.scholastic.co.uk     **PHOTOCOPIABLE**                                   **Scholastic Literacy Skills**
**Grammar and punctuation: Year 5**   **53**

Name:

**Nouns, pronouns and writing**

# She did what?

■ Using the words below, can you make mini-stories one sentence long? For example: *He found her.* What could the story be about? What ideas does it give for longer story writing?

| | |
|---|---|
| I | me |
| he | him |
| she | her |
| it | them |
| they | it |
| lost | made |
| found | saw |

**PHOTOCOPIABLE**

# Clauses

## Introduction

It may seem odd to give a whole chapter over to one aspect of grammar; however, the activities in this chapter introduce clauses, taking children through one of the most awkward themes of grammar that they will encounter in Key Stage 2.

## Poster notes

### Clauses and sentences (page 56)

The definitions and examples on this poster are not enough to clarify the different ways clauses can feature in sentences. The poster is therefore a reference point for the teacher to explain the idea. 'Main clauses' and 'Clauses in sentences' contain ideas to develop children's understanding of this area.

### Connectives (page 57)

This poster presents the functions of connectives. It can form a useful companion to poster page 102 'Connectives' where a range of connectives are gathered.

## In this chapter

| | |
|---|---|
| **Main clauses** page 58 | Identify the main clause in a sentence. |
| **Clauses in sentences** page 62 | Investigate sentences that contain more than one clause. |
| **Connectives** page 66 | Understand how clauses are connected. |
| **Using connectives** page 70 | Use connectives to link clauses and sentences. |
| **Experimenting with clauses in writing** page 74 | Apply learning about clauses to writing. |

# Clauses

## Clauses and sentences

### Complex

sentences contain a main clause and a subordinate clause.

The cat woke up because the dog barked.

### Compound

sentences contain clauses of equal importance.

The cat slept and the dog ate.

### Simple

sentences contain one clause:

The cat slept.

# Clauses

# CONNECTIVES

Oppose one clause with another

for example, I like rain **but** my friend hates it.

Show how one clause is linked by time to another

for example, we put on warm clothes **then** we went out in the snow.

Add one clause to another

for example, I like rain **and** I like snow.

Show how one clause is caused by another

for example, I like snow **because** it looks great.

*Illustrations © 2008, Moreno Chiacchiera/Beehive Illustration.*

# Main clauses

## Objective

Identify the main clause in a sentence.

## Background knowledge

Clauses are units of language that make sense in themselves. They can be *whole* sentences, such as *The cat slept*, or they can feature *within* sentences. Within sentences they feature as distinct elements with verbs of their own. In a sentence like *The cat slept even though the orchestra played, because they didn't disturb it*, there are three distinct clauses:

    'The cat slept'
    'the orchestra played'
    'they didn't disturb it'.
    Each of these clauses could make a discrete, short sentence. In this sentence the 'main clause' is 'The cat slept', while the other two provide information about the cat sleeping, and are therefore 'subordinate clauses'.

## Activities

As a means of reinforcing the concept of clauses to the class, these activities ask children to look for the main clause in lengthy sentences. As they do this, children need to bear in mind that a main clause is very much like a sentence in itself.

● **Photocopiable page 59 'What is the sentence about?'**
As children undertake this activity, one way of focusing upon the main clause in each sentence is to ask what the main event is in each of the examples given.

● **Photocopiable page 60 'Find the main clause'**
This activity involves children trimming sentences to isolate the main clause. Once they have done this they can also look at the elements of the sentence left over, asking themselves what job these do and seeing if they can find leftovers that have something in common (such as explaining why an event occurred).

● **Photocopiable page 61 'Sentence repairs'**
In this activity children match the clauses together to rebuild a broken sentence. Once they have done this, they could reflect on which parts of the rebuilt sentence can stand independently. For example, in *Shona had a leaving party so that we could all say 'Goodbye' to her*, the first half of the sentence makes sense on its own: 'Shona had a leaving party' whereas the second half does not: 'so that we could all say 'Goodbye' to her'. The first half is the main clause. The second half is a subordinate clause that explains the reason behind the party.

## Further ideas

● **Roundabout way of saying:** Children could try to devise their own sentences in the style of the examples shown on photocopiable page 59 'What is the sentence about?' They can try to find a plain sentence and to create a long, flowery version of the same thing.
● **Plain words:** Ask children to find examples of flowery ways of saying something, either in material that they have read or that their parents have received. Junk mail makes an excellent starting point for this, as it tends to be verbose while saying very little!

## What's on the CD-ROM

On the CD-ROM you will find:
● Printable versions of all three photocopiable pages.
● Answers to all three photocopiable pages.
● Interactive versions of all three photocopiable pages.

## Main clauses

# What is the sentence about?

■ Here are some very long sentences. Can you write a shorter sentence that says the main thing from the bigger sentence? You might remove bits from:

| the beginning | or the middle | or the end |
|---|---|---|
| Realising I had nothing else to do for the time being, I played with my friend. | I, having thought and thought about what I could do to fill a space of time available to me, played with my friend. | I played with my friend because I really, really wanted to, more than anything else in the world. |

I played with my friend.

■ Write your shortened sentences in the space provided.

| Long version | Shortened version |
|---|---|
| The tree, which for many years had stood outside the school gate beside the road, fell over. | The tree fell over. |
| As part of an assembly to celebrate the start of the new school year, Caroline sang a song. | |
| Before visiting us to celebrate my birthday, my Uncle made a cake. | |
| I played with my friend, which is hardly surprising, because I do that every day after school. | |
| It was, without any shadow of a doubt, raining. | |
| Sam swallowed his tooth, although he was not made ill by this accident. | |
| The caretaker mended our window which is good because it was broken and needed mending. | |
| There was, during the afternoon of Thursday the 1st of September, a thunderstorm. | |

Name:

## Main clauses

# Find the main clause

In long sentences there is usually a main clause. It is the main thing the sentence is about. In a sentence like:

> The cat slept, even though the orchestra played, because they didn't disturb it.

the main clause is

> The cat slept

The other bits of the sentence add more information about the main clause.

> the orchestra played

> they didn't disturb it

Main clauses sometimes look like little sentences inside bigger sentences.

■ Cut out each main clause from these sentences.

| After tea my mum watches telly because she likes the news. |
|---|
| The boy fell off the swing although he wasn't injured. |
| I saw a good film at the cinema that I hadn't seen before. |
| If it's open we are going to the library so that we can change our books. |
| I am watching the kettle until it boils. |
| Open the window so that we can get some fresh air. |
| It is time to clear up unless you want to stay in after school. |
| When the bell rings we can go out to play unless it is raining. |

**PHOTOCOPIABLE**   ■SCHOLASTIC
www.scholastic.co.uk

## Main clauses

# Sentence repairs

■ Match the beginnings and endings of the sentences below.

| | |
|---|---|
| Without checking he had his bus fare | my brother wore his wet trainers. |
| The classroom was messy | Sam ran to catch the bus. |
| It was sunny | so our teacher was not pleased. |
| We made sandwiches | until we changed at half time. |
| By next Tuesday | so that we could all say 'Goodbye' to her. |
| After thinking about it for ages | my bike will be mended. |
| Because of the rain | my Dad decided to have a hair cut. |
| Even after he had been told not to | because we were having a picnic. |
| Shona had a leaving party | although the forecast predicted rain. |
| Ali was in goal | our trip was cancelled. |

# Clauses in sentences

## Objective

Investigate sentences that contain more than one clause.

## Background knowledge

Sentences can feature various combinations of clauses of different types.

● **Simple sentences:** contain one clause, such as *The cat slept.*

● **Compound sentences:** contain more than one clause. In compound sentences the clauses are of equal importance. Each clause is like a sentence in itself and neither can be picked out as the main clause: *The cat slept and the dog ate* or *The dog ate and the cat slept and the hamster knitted and the fish dived.*

● **Complex sentences:** have a main clause and a subordinate clause, the latter being, in some way, dependent upon the main clause in order to make sense: *The cat woke up because the dog barked.*

## Activities

The main focus of these activities should be the distinguishing and picking apart of one clause from another. This can involve looking at different types of clause.

● **Photocopiable page 63 'Two clauses'**
In this activity children are asked to separate the two clauses in a sentence. Remind them that one way of doing this is by locating the verbs in a sentence. Remind them that clauses are like mini-sentences. Once they have completed the activity, they can look at the way in which some clauses are subordinate to others.

● **Photocopiable page 64 'Create a complexity'**
Using various clauses, this activity requires children to create obscure sentences. They can add capital letters and full stops to these and keep a record of some of the more difficult constructions they devise.

● **Photocopiable page 65 'The sub-clause'**
This activity asks children to look at the sub-clause in various sentences. It is worth remembering that a main clause is one that can stand on its own whereas a sub-clause is dependent upon the main clause to make sense.

## Further ideas

● **Most clauses:** Children can look in texts available in the classroom with the challenge of trying to find the sentence that contains the greatest number of clauses.

● **Cutting out sentences:** Using disposable texts, such as leaflets and adverts, children can cut up the sentences they find into separate clauses.

● **Sentence shuffle:** Children can try making their own sets of clauses like the ones used on photocopiable page 64 'Create a complexity'. The key thing here is to include some wayward and obscure clauses so that when the shuffling around takes place strange sentences start to appear.

## What's on the CD-ROM

On the CD-ROM you will find:
● Printable versions of all three photocopiable pages.
● Answers to 'Two clauses' and 'The sub-clause'.
● Interactive versions of 'Create a complexity' and 'The sub-clause'.

**Clauses in sentences**

# Two clauses

- Each of these sentences contains two clauses.
- Write each clause in the spaces underneath the sentence.

The car stopped because it ran out of petrol.

After we finished dinner, we went out to play.

Ahmed is seven today so we are having a party.

I like lemonade but my mum can't stand it.

Name:

## Clauses in sentences

# Create a complexity

■ Using the clauses below, make up some long and strange sentences – for example, *My dog fell off the wall because of my Granny's teeth.*

■ Put in the correct punctuation for each of your sentences.

| | |
|---|---|
| my dog fell off the wall | the burglar ran away |
| my mum was sad | at a café beside the sea |
| and they went all over the table | because she spun round and round |
| when she saw a cat | because of my Granny's teeth |
| which she lost at Cleethorpes | while eating a bowl of cornflakes |
| while scratching his fleas | inside the teacher's desk |
| in the middle of the night | Aunty Louisa sneezed |
| with a jam sponge | I fell in the pool |
| which really belonged to my neighbour | wearing a pair of bright green trunks |
| so that he wouldn't get caught | and she started to cry |

## Clauses in sentences

# The sub-clause

■ Read each of the sentences below. Write the words that make up sub-clauses in the boxes.

My mum, who's a vet, works in the city.

Josh found, after trying and trying, he could swim a whole length.

The children made a cake because they were having a party.

If you want a good laugh, you should read my story.

After writing their stories, the children made a play.

The girl looked for her shoes, having lost them in the classroom.

If the weather improves we can play rounders.

When the clock says three o'clock, we can pack up for home time.

Before going into assembly, we have to line up.

Our teacher, a very scruffy man, wore a tie today.

# Connectives

## Objective

Understand how clauses are connected.

## Background knowledge

Clauses can be connected together in various ways in order to make a simple into a complex or compound sentence. Connections can indicate the relationship between two clauses. The main connections involve:

● **Addition:** one clause adding information to another, linked by words like 'and' and 'also' – such as *The dog barked and the cat ran.*

● **Opposition:** one clause contradicting or standing in opposition to another, linked by words like 'but', 'yet' and 'though' – such as *The dog barked but the cat stayed asleep.*

● **Cause:** one clause caused by another, linked by words like 'because' and 'therefore' – such as *The cat woke up because the dog barked.*

● **Time:** one clause in a temporal relationship with another, linked by words like 'then' and 'after' – such as *The dog barked then the cat woke up.*

## Activities

As they encounter the various connectives in these activities, children should familiarise themselves with the use of various words to connect clauses. This involves having some idea of the different ways in which clauses can be connected.

● **Photocopiable page 67 'Choose the connective'**
As they create sentences using the parts shown on the photocopiable sheet, children have to consider the most appropriate connective to link two clauses. This will involve understanding the relationship between the two clauses and finding an appropriate word.

● **Photocopiable page 68 'Find the connectives'**
Using their awareness of the different functions performed by connectives, children can sort the sentences shown into four groups according to whether the connectives make their link using addition, opposition, cause or time. To begin the task children should locate and circle the connective.

● **Photocopiable page 69 'Use the connective'**
This activity presents a wider range of connectives that children can try to use in sentences of their own devising.

## Further ideas

● **Analysing leaflets:** Collect information leaflets from a variety of sources and ask children to read through them to find the different connective words that are used.

● **New connective:** The class can choose a connective to promote. They can try to slip it into their speech and writing. For example, they could adopt the word 'furthermore' then they have to use it as often as possible.

● **Find other ones:** Looking through various texts, children can try to find new connectives and keep a list of them. These could also be classified according to the function they perform.

## What's on the CD-ROM

On the CD-ROM you will find:
● Printable versions of all three photocopiable pages.
● Answers to 'Choose the connective' and 'Find the connectives'.
● Interactive version of 'Find the connectives'.

## Connectives

# Choose the connective

■ Look at the sentence parts below. Choose starters, connectives and finishers that fit together and make sentences. Write them below.

■ Make up your own sentences using a starter, a connective and a finisher.

| Starters | Connective | Finishers |
|---|---|---|
| I like football | but | I had my tea. |
| First I went home | and | the water had boiled. |
| I went to the park | also | I don't like cricket. |
| I set out for school | after | my friend came too. |
| We went to the fair | then | she moans too much. |
| Our teacher is grumpy | so that | I could buy a new game. |
| I saved my pocket money | because | I had finished my breakfast. |
| The steam came out of the kettle | although | the roller coaster was closed. |

Name:

## Connectives

# Find the connectives

Connectives are words or phrases that link parts of a text together. They are often used to connect clauses.

| Addition | Opposition | Cause | Time |
|---|---|---|---|
| Add one clause to another. | Show one clause opposes another. | Show how one clause is caused by another. | Show how one clause is linked to the time of another. |
| For example: I like rain **and** I like snow. | For example: I like sun **but** I hate rain. | For example: I like snow **because** it looks great. | For example: We put on warm clothes **then** went out in the snow. |

- ■ Sort these sentences according to the job the connective is doing.
- ■ Remember, the connective can come anywhere in the sentence.

| |
|---|
| We did some writing after we finished art. |
| The television made a noise because it was broken. |
| We are going swimming and we are going skating. |
| We were going to go out but we had to tidy up. |
| The children lined up before going into school. |
| The hinges are loose so the door won't open. |
| The roof is leaking, also the window is broken. |
| I thought we were doing art, but we are doing PE. |
| We'll have to tidy up, which means we'll miss playtime. |
| The water boiled and the toast popped out of the toaster. |

## Connectives

# Use the connective

■ Write a sentence using each of the connectives shown in the table below.

| Connective | Sentence |
| --- | --- |
| so that | We will switch on the heating so that we can be warm. |
| because | |
| then | |
| and also | |
| furthermore | |
| consequently | |
| as a result | |
| on the other hand | |
| meanwhile | |
| but | |
| instead of | |

# Using connectives

## Objective

Use connectives to link clauses and sentences.

## Background knowledge

Clauses can be connected using various words and phrases (as well as punctuation features such as colons and commas). When it comes to words and phrases, the connectives used will vary according to the relationship between clauses. In a compound sentence (one in which the clauses are of equal importance) the connecting words will tend to be words like 'and' or 'then'. In a complex sentence the connecting words will subordinate one clause to another, making one the explanation of another, with words like 'because' and 'therefore'.

## Activities

Children should expand the number of connectives they can draw upon in their own writing by examining their use in sentences. Care should be taken to avoid any idea that longer sentences are inherently better. Children need to be aware that they are being given the ability to construct these, should they be of use. However, a short sentence can be just as useful in the right context.

Connectives form one of the main ways in which a text has cohesion. Different text types tend to draw a lot on particular connecting words. A narrative text will draw upon temporal connectives whereas an explanatory text may draw upon causal connectives in constructing explanations.

● **Photocopiable page 71 'Same start, different ending…'**
Using the different connectives should cause children to produce different sentence endings. The various sentences can be discussed to examine how the function of the connectives steered the various sentences in particular ways.

● **Photocopiable page 72 'Connecting words'**
This activity asks children to seek out the connectives in a story from Terry Jones's *Fairy Tales*. This could lead to a discussion of the function the connectives perform. Note that this activity points out connectives working within and across sentences. Connectives used in the story: 'and', 'but', 'so', 'therefore', 'before'.

● **Photocopiable page 73 'Short and long sentences'**
Drawing on a selection of short, single-clause sentences, children are asked to create longer, complex and compound examples. One aspect of this activity worth following up is the use of connectives. Children will use various connectives depending on the relationship between the clauses.

## Further ideas

● **Connective challenge:** Challenge the children to produce a sentence that uses four different connectives. They should each be performing one of the functions of connectives.

● **Text marking:** Using leaflets and cuttings, children can find connectives and circle them, then draw links joining them to the clauses and sentences they join.

 **What's on the CD-ROM**

On the CD-ROM you will find:
● Printable versions of all three photocopiable pages.

## Using connectives

# Same start, different ending...

■ Using the sentence starters below, complete the sentences. The first one is done for you.

■ How does the connective affect the way you finish the sentence?

| | |
|---|---|
| The girl opened the box after | *the postman had given it to her.* |
| The girl opened the box so that | |
| The girl opened the box and | |
| The girl opened the box but | |

| | |
|---|---|
| We enjoy playtime but | |
| We enjoy playtime, on the other hand | |
| We enjoy playtime because | |
| We enjoy playtime after | |

| | |
|---|---|
| The magician appeared when | |
| The magician appeared in order that | |
| The magician appeared meanwhile | |
| The magician appeared and also | |

**SCHOLASTIC**
www.scholastic.co.uk     **PHOTOCOPIABLE**                                **Scholastic Literacy Skills**
                                                           Grammar and punctuation: Year 5    **71**

Name:

# Connecting words

Connecting words can make links within sentences.

They can also make links across sentences, linking one sentence

| We had our tea. |
| --- |

with another

| We had our tea. | After that | we played outside |
| --- | --- | --- |

■ Look for the connecting words in this story. What function is each of them performing?

### Three Raindrops

A raindrop was falling out of a cloud, and it said to the raindrop next to it: 'I'm the biggest and best raindrop in the whole sky!'

'You are indeed a fine raindrop,' said the second, 'but you are not nearly so beautifully shaped as I am. And in my opinion it's shape that counts, and *I* am therefore the best raindrop in the whole sky.'

The first raindrop replied: 'Let us settle this matter once and for all.' So they asked a third raindrop to decide between them.

But the third raindrop said: 'What nonsense you're both talking! *You* may be a big raindrop, and *you* are certainly well shaped, but, as everybody knows, it's purity that really counts, and I am purer than either of you. *I* am therefore the best raindrop in the whole sky!'

Well, before either of the other raindrops could reply, they all three hit the ground and became part of a very muddy puddle.

*Terry Jones*

**PHOTOCOPIABLE**

**SCHOLASTIC**
www.scholastic.co.uk

## Using connectives

# Short and long sentences

■ Look at these short sentences.

| | | | |
|---|---|---|---|
| We are not happy. | We helped the dinner supervisors. | We will show our parents. | We are working together. |
| We can't go outside. | We have nearly finished. | We are making a display. | We co-operated. |
| We have to tidy up. | The bell rang. | We are working very hard. | We go to dinner. |
| Our teacher asked us to help. | We didn't finish our work. | We are enjoying ourselves. | We finished our work. |
| It is raining outside. | We are practising a play. | We finished our pictures. | We are waiting for the bell. |

■ Use these short sentences as clauses in longer sentences. Try using two short sentences to make each long sentence. You can use any connecting words needed between the clauses, for example:

> We helped the dinner supervisors until the bell rang.

_____

_____

_____

_____

_____

_____

# Experimenting with clauses in writing

## Objective

Apply learning about clauses to writing.

## Writing focus

Understanding and reflecting on clauses can be a vital way of improving individual sentences in writing. It's through experimenting with clauses, adding to them and qualifying them, that children can learn to enrich the individual sentence.

## Skills to writing

● **Focus on the clause**

The clause is one of the single most important tools for developing children's writing. From a basic sentence they can develop a connection that elaborates their expression in writing. Children need to get used to looking at simple sentences and asking whether more could be added.

● **Ice the cake**

One way of developing the above is to ask the children if they can revise a sentence they have written, like putting the icing on the cake to make it even more appealing. If they have written *I went to the park*, can they think why they went, or something interesting about the journey? For example: *I was so bored that I went to the park* or *I went to the park even though it was raining*.

● **Clause hunting**

Encourage children to revisit their writing, seeking out the number of clauses they have used in each sentence. Ask them to look for those parts of a long sentence that could have stood as sentences in their own right. While doing this, encourage them to also look out for sentences where another clause could be added to qualify their original one.

● **Connectives in non-fiction**

Take note of the sort of connectives used in non-fiction texts. This can include looking at the use of causal connectives in explanatory texts, oppositional connectives in argument texts and temporal connectives in narrative. It can also expand to include a look at the stylistic features of certain well-known texts, such as the sort of connective that dominates football reports or instructions for playing a game. They can also listen out for the type of connective used in well-known performances, such as the 'set pieces' of comedians. For example, the comedian whose portrayal of a stroppy teenager involves a heap of causal connectives that interweave the character's complex explanation of something. The experience of listening and picking apart sentences can attune children to their structure.

● **Gobbledegook prize**

Encourage children to seek out the most complex printed sentence they can find. It can be one with loads of different clauses, variously connected, with commas and conjunctions everywhere. Set a challenge to find the most complex example.

## Activities

● **Photocopiable page 76 'Connective dice'**

Ask the children to cut out the cube nets and turn them into dice. The idea is that they use these alongside a piece of writing, about a paragraph long. Taking their paragraph, they roll the dice and see whether they can use one of the two connectives that appear. Children could work in twos, setting themselves a challenge of sharing in the revision of a piece of writing, trying to find a use for a connective on each throw of the dice.

● **Photocopiable page 77 'Inserting clauses'**

This activity encourages children to lengthen sentences to ridiculous degrees. They may wish to write their additions in various coloured felt-tipped pens to give the whole thing a bit of colour.

## Write on

### ● One-sentence stories

Challenge the children to come up with a whole story in one sentence. This is different from the days when they didn't use full stops because they didn't know how to use them. Now, using a skilled combination of commas and connectives, children need to produce a story that extends a simple sentence into a convoluted set of events: *The Princess married the prince* becomes *Even though he was a frog, the Princess married the prince* and *Even though he was a frog, and despite the efforts of the bad fairy who tried to stop the wedding, the Princess married the prince.* Add an 'although' at the end and the story is getting more complex.

### ● Oppositions

These are old music hall skits that can be adapted for the classroom. The idea used to be to tell a story that went from good to bad, then to good and back to bad.

> *They're building a house.*
> *It's a school house.*
> *It's only got one classroom.*
> *It's a mile long.*

The audience could boo and cheer each line as it went along. Children could try creating their own announcement of a similar nature, maybe about school closing or playtimes.

### ● Explain routines

Children often use explanation writing in scientific or geographical contexts, but they also have a place in PSHE. It's here that children can devise their own reasoning for certain rules and routines around the school – why do we only have a short playtime? Taking some of the less popular school rules and routines children can be asked to try exploring the reasoning behind them (whether or not they agree with the resultant rule) and turn this into an explanation.

### ● Comma and

Devise sentences with certain patterns to them. One example is the 'comma and', with two clauses separated by a comma then a third following 'and'. *I put on my shoes, I grabbed my coat and I ran out the door.* At first the model will lead to forced examples, but children start to both take on the rhythm of sentences and take structures from other complex sentences to adapt for their own content.

### What's on the CD-ROM

On the CD-ROM you will find:
- Printable versions of both photocopiable pages.
- Interactive version of 'Connective dice'.

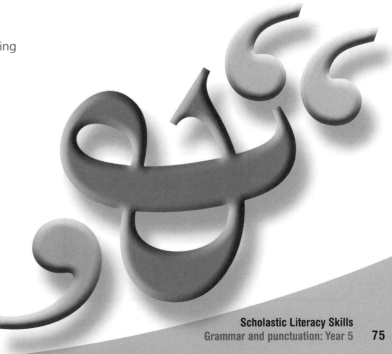

Name:

# Connective dice

■ Make two dice using these nets. Roll the dice while you are writing and see what connectives you land on. Can you use them in your text?

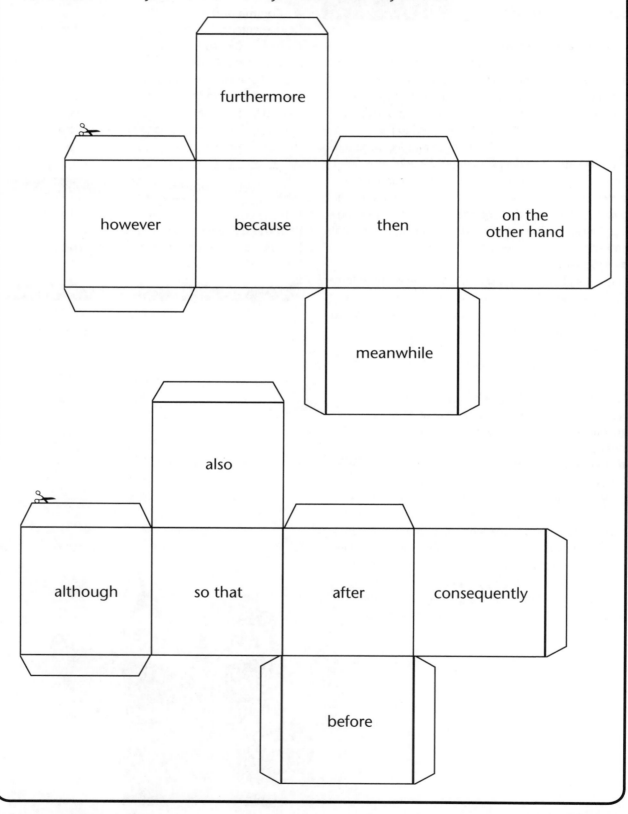

furthermore

however | because | then | on the other hand

meanwhile

also

although | so that | after | consequently

before

**PHOTOCOPIABLE**

**Experimenting with clauses in writing**

# Inserting clauses

■ Cut up these simple sentences. Make clauses to extend them. Write these new clauses on strips of paper and tape them into the simple sentence. For example:

Could become

or

| I am going home. | I will make you a drink. |
|---|---|
| I like cheese. | I told them. |

**PHOTOCOPIABLE**

*Illustrations © 2008, Moreno Chiacchiera/Beehive Illustration.*

# Chapter 4

# Prepositions and punctuation

## Introduction

The small class of words called *prepositions* performs essential tasks in the English language. Prepositions are introduced in this chapter. They tend to be relatively easy to identify and children quickly grasp their function. The chapter also includes work on apostrophes of possession and punctuation.

## Poster notes

**Prepositions (page 79)**
This poster provides a list of common prepositions.

**Playtime (page 80)**
This poster is designed to stimulate children's talk about prepositions. As they look across the poster, can they see people and things that are on, under and next to other things? As they work with prepositions, it provides a resource to which they can refer.

## In this chapter

| | |
|---|---|
| **Introducing prepositions** page 81 | Identify prepositions. |
| **Understanding prepositions** page 85 | Experiment with a range of prepositions. |
| **Using prepositions** page 89 | Experiment with the use of prepositions. |
| **Word order** page 93 | Investigate word order and key words, looking at the alteration of sentences. |
| **Writing prepositions** page 97 | Use a range of prepositions to enhance precision in writing. |

# PREPOSITIONS

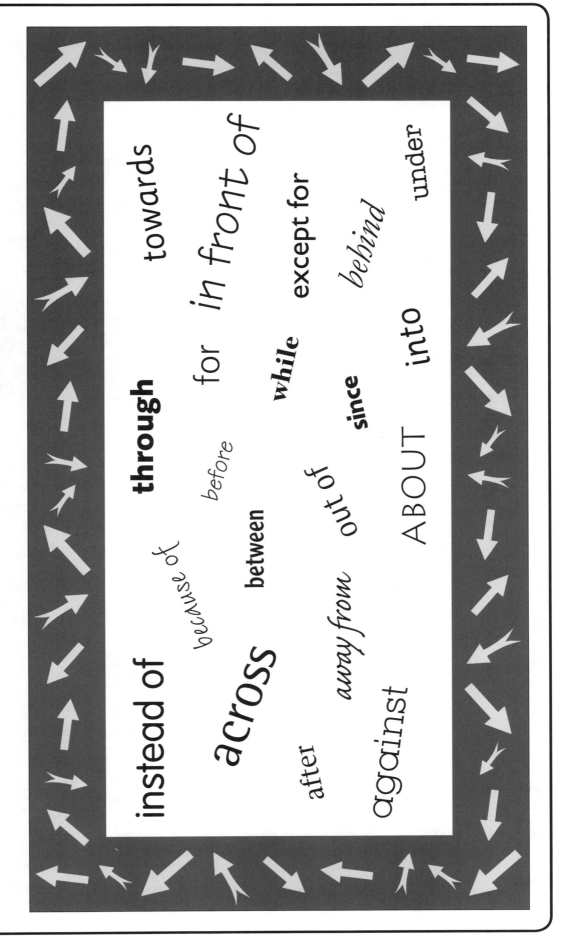

towards

in front of

for

except for

behind

under

through

before

while

since

into

because of

between

out of

ABOUT

instead of

across

after

away from

against

**Prepositions and punctuation**

# Playtime

Write **eight** sentences describing parts of this scene. Try using a range of prepositions.

Illustrations © 2008, Moreno Chiacchiera/Beehive Illustration.

# Introducing prepositions

## Objective

Identify prepositions.

## Background knowledge

Prepositions are words or phrases that indicate when or where something is in relation to something else. They are, as the word implies, position words that come before other words. They usually appear before a noun or a pronoun. In a sentence like *The cow jumped over the moon* the preposition 'over' explains where the cow jumped in relation to the moon (as opposed to 'under' or 'through' it). There is a limited number of prepositions in the English language. A survey of words that have been added to the language will show a growth in certain word types such as nouns and verbs. The number of prepositions, on the other hand, tends to remain stable.

## Activities

The crucial aspect of work on prepositions is to enable children to identify them. They will use most of them already, and will be able to read and write many. In these activities they identify the prepositions they know.

● **Photocopiable page 82 'Listing prepositions'**
This activity asks children to list all the prepositions they can think of. As they do this you may wish to let them look in various texts such as story books, newspapers and instruction leaflets in order to find examples.

● **Photocopiable page 83 'Find the prepositions'**
Looking at the text, children have to find the prepositions. Remind them that prepositions are about more than just place – they can indicate time as well.

● **Photocopiable page 84 'The drawing game'**
Ask the children to work in pairs. One should be the leader and the other the follower. The leader draws a route from the start to the finish of the strip. They can be fairly elaborate about this, going back on themselves, up and down and through the shapes, but they must not let the follower see their route. Once the leader has completed their route they have to sit so that they cannot see the follower's strip and vice versa. They then have to use directions to instruct the follower how to get from start to finish, using the same line. This will involve using prepositions, for example, 'over', 'between', 'around'. Once the route is complete, they can compare strips to see how well the follower did.

## Further ideas

● **The exhaustive guide:** The class can turn their own efforts at preposition recognition into a whole-class list to which they all contribute.
● **Dictionary hunting:** Ask the children to work in groups, looking through the dictionary a page at a time finding any prepositions they can. This may add to the list being drawn up by the class.
● **Shared reading:** The book *Rosie's Walk* by Pat Hutchins (Red Fox) is an ever-popular children's story. It also provides an entertaining example of a story that uses a range of prepositions in describing Rosie's walk across and through various features of the farmyard.

## What's on the CD-ROM

On the CD-ROM you will find:
● Printable versions of all three photocopiable pages.
● Answers to 'Find the prepositions'.
● Interactive version of 'Find the prepositions'.

Name:

# Listing prepositions

Prepositions are words that can show the link between two things.

- They could be linked in time for example:

I had breakfast before school.

- or space

Put the jigsaw in the box.

- or in another way

This cake is for Gran.

■ How many prepositions can you think of? Write them down.

**PHOTOCOPIABLE**

**SCHOLASTIC**
www.scholastic.co.uk

**Introducing prepositions**

# Find the prepositions

■ Can you find the prepositions in these directions?

Travel by boat up the river towards the windmill. Stop beside the windmill and walk behind it. Walk across the field into the wood. Carefully pass through the wood until you see the arch. Before going through the archway check you are not being followed. Go under the arch and through the tunnel. You will come out by the old oak tree. After reaching the oak tree walk down the hill and over the stream. Near the stream you will see a house on a hill. Go to the door, the key is under the mat, and step inside...

Name:

**Introducing prepositions**

# The drawing game

■  Draw a route from start to finish on the top half of the sheet. Then describe it to your partner. Use the bottom half of the sheet to draw the route your partner describes.

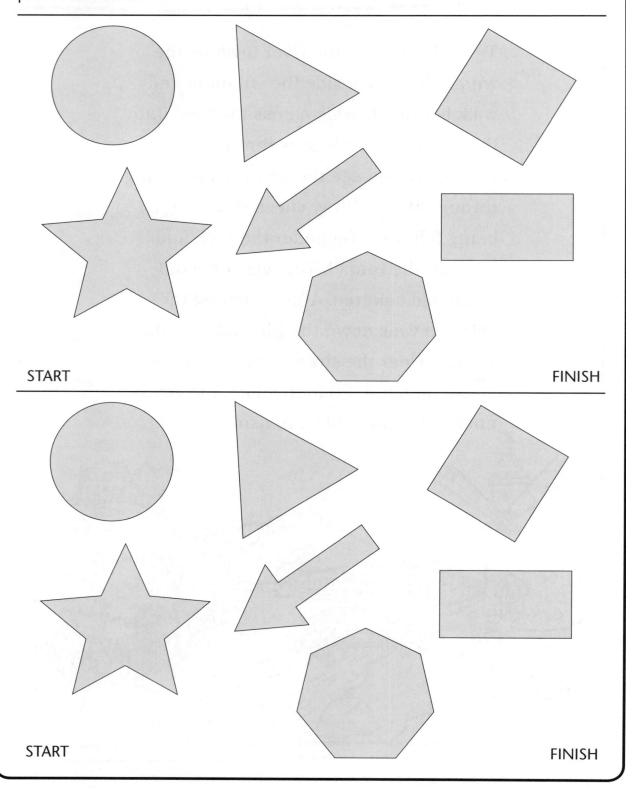

START                                                                                    FINISH

START                                                                                    FINISH

PHOTOCOPIABLE

**■SCHOLASTIC**
www.scholastic.co.uk

# Understanding prepositions

## Objective

Experiment with a range of prepositions.

## Background knowledge

Prepositions are crucial words in relating the links between grammatical ideas. They tend to be short words, and are limited in number. Prepositions can consist of one word, such as 'over', 'at', or 'before' or two words, such as 'out of' and 'away from'. There are also complex prepositions that are made up of three words, such as 'in front of' and 'on top of'.

## Activities

Prepositions constitute a limited category of words rarely added to. However, there is a range of words here that children can develop and expand in their own writing.

● **Photocopiable page 86 'Preposition cutting'**
One way of approaching the task of identifying a class of words within a sentence is to eliminate other classes. In this activity children cut out any nouns, verbs and so on, leaving behind words they think are prepositions.

● **Photocopiable page 87 'Preposition spaces'**
This cloze activity will involve children in examining the context of the story in order to decide which preposition best fits the newspaper article.

● **Photocopiable page 88 'Using prepositions'**
This activity asks children to produce sentences that use a range of prepositions. It can be made more challenging by suggesting to children that, as they write their sentences, they may include another preposition not shown on the photocopiable sheet.

## Further ideas

● **Preposition cards:** Write some prepositions on a set of ten cards. Ask children to place the cards face down and take turns at removing three cards from the pile and making a sentence with whichever prepositions they select.
● **Word count:** Children can sort the various prepositions they find and use according to the number of words they contain. For example: one word – 'over'; two words – 'out of' and three words – 'on top of'.

## What's on the CD-ROM

On the CD-ROM you will find:
● Printable versions of all three photocopiable pages.
● Answers to 'Preposition cutting'
● Interactive versions of all three photocopiable pages.

Name:

**Understanding prepositions**

# Preposition cutting

■ Read these sentences carefully. Cross out all the words that are **not** prepositions. Make a list of the prepositions you are left with.

_____

Gran left her bicycle against the railings in front of the library.

_____

She went into the library and, as far
as she was concerned, the bike was safely parked outside.

_____

After half an hour she came out of the library.

_____

Alongside the railings there was nothing except for the bicycle pump.

_____

Gran looked all around and saw someone riding away on her bike.

_____

She ran after the thief and caught up with him near to the market.

_____

In spite of the fact he was twice as big as her, she ran
towards him and knocked him off the bike with the pump.

_____

He jumped over the wall and ran off through the market.

_____

**PHOTOCOPIABLE**

**■SCHOLASTIC**
www.scholastic.co.uk

_Illustrations © 2008, Moreno Chiacchiera/Beehive Illustration._

# Preposition spaces

■ Look at the newspaper article below. Prepositions have been removed from the text. Can you think of a word that would fit each of the spaces? Remember, prepositions can be one or two words or more.

# Hands _____ the water

_____ weeks _____ preparation, Martina Hands, a teacher _____ Balstone Junior, is ready _____ a challenging ordeal. Martina plans to sail _____ the English Channel _____ a home-made raft. The raft is made _____ recycled materials and has been trialled _____ all types of water, _____ the Channel. This Saturday raft and Channel meet for the first time, battling _____ themselves to see who will win. Martina is confident the raft will hold _____ wind and rain. She will be protected _____ a tarpaulin but says she will still wrap up well.

Martina has always been a keen sailor. _____ teaching she was _____ the navy. She said "I've been _____ difficult journeys and am looking forward _____ this one. But I hope I'm not _____ school for too long."

# Boxing match

Fruit seller, Carl Hall, is furious _____ council plans to stop his long-standing practice of stacking fruit boxes _____ his shop. Council officials say his boxes are obstructing the pavement, where they are arranged. "I am furious," said Carl. "I have displayed goods _____ the canopy _____ my shop _____ years and _____ this I have never had any complaints." Pointing to the pavement he says "There is plenty of room _____ boxes and the road. I can't see what all the fuss is _____."

Council spokesperson said "Mr Hall has ample room to display goods _____ his shop window. We don't want a fuss _____ a couple of boxes." But Carl plans to appeal _____ the council's decision.

Name:

# Using prepositions

■ Write sentences in the spaces provided, using both the prepositions.

| | |
|---|---|
| instead of | Instead of just standing beside it, we jumped into the pool. |
| into | |
| except for | |
| about | |
| away from | |
| between | |
| across | |
| because of | |
| in front of | |
| before | |
| through | |
| after | |
| against | |
| since | |
| towards | |
| out of | |
| while | |
| behind | |
| under | |
| for | |

# Using prepositions

## Objective

Experiment with the use of prepositions.

## Background knowledge

Two of the most significant functions of prepositions are to show relationships of space, such as 'over' and 'near', or time, such as 'before' and 'after'. Prepositions can also indicate possession (*The house of my uncle*) or they can show other links between nouns (*I want coffee instead of tea*).

## Activities

Prepositions are relatively bland words. Nevertheless, there is some consideration to be given to which ones are best used in particular contexts. Throughout these activities children explore the range of prepositions they could use in a variety of ways.

● **Photocopiable page 90 'Possible prepositions'**
Certain prepositions perform certain tasks. Looking at the context in these sentences children can try figuring out what job could be performed by which prepositions.

● **Photocopiable page 91 'Preposition diary'**
This activity revises the use of prepositions to place things temporally. The children can try to use each of the examples shown.

● **Photocopiable page 92 'Pop'**
Using Michael Rosen's poem 'Busy Day' as a guide to preposition use, children can use various imperatives to produce their own poem in a similar vein.

## Further ideas

● **Big pictures:** Try and obtain a large picture in which a lot is taking place, such as a modern cartoon poster or a print of a classic picture (Brueghel's *Children's Games* is good for this). Ask children to point out things and notice how they use prepositions.

● **Comic stories:** Looking at three pictures from a comic story, ask children to write sentences about the scenes using a variety of prepositions. Remind them that they can write using time prepositions ('before', 'after') as well as spatial ones ('over', 'through').

● **Directions:** Make a tape recording of an adult giving directions. Replay the tape and note the prepositions used. Which ones are the most common?

##  What's on the CD-ROM

On the CD-ROM you will find:
● Printable versions of all three photocopiable pages.
● Interactive version of 'Possible prepositions'.

Name:

**Using prepositions**

# Possible prepositions

■ Look at these sentences and list **two** prepositions that could fill the spaces.

Wash the paint pots _____ playtime.

The football was _____ the shelf.

I found my pencil _____ the book.

You can use a pencil _____ a pen.

Put the bottle _____ the sink.

I met Joe _____ the library.

We had something to eat _____ playing outside.

**PHOTOCOPIABLE**

■SCHOLASTIC
www.scholastic.co.uk

**Using prepositions**

# Preposition diary

Prepositions tell us
- where things are in relation to each other
- when things happened in relation to each other.

■ Write a diary of your day, using prepositions. Think of something that happened before something else, or after something else. For example:

| | | | |
|---|---|---|---|
| I did exercises before breakfast. | During the news I tidied the room. | After tea I played outside. | I played outside for half the afternoon. |

■ Prepositions to use:

| while before since after for during while around until |
|---|

Illustrations © 2008, Moreno Chiacchiera/Beehive Illustration.

**Using prepositions**

# Pop

■ Read this poem by Michael Rosen.

■ Notice how many different prepositions are used. Could you write a similar poem, using a range of prepositions after a verb?

**Busy Day**

Pop in
pop out
pop over the road
pop out for a walk
pop in for a talk
pop down to the shop
can't stop
got to pop

got to pop?

pop where?
pop what?

well
I've got to
pop round
pop up
pop in to town
pop out and see
pop in for tea
pop down to the shop
can't stop
got to pop

got to pop?

pop where?
pop what?

well
I've got to
pop in
pop out
pop over the road
pop out for a walk
pop in for a talk.....

*Michael Rosen*

**PHOTOCOPIABLE**      **■SCHOLASTIC**
www.scholastic.co.uk

# Word order

## Objective

Investigate word order and key words, looking at the alteration of sentences.

## Background knowledge

Within a sentence, words can be classified as 'content' words or 'function' words.

● **Content words:** as their name implies, carry the content of communication. In a sentence like *The man bit a dog* the two participants ('man', 'dog') and the action ('bit') make up the content of the communication. The two other words are functional. They relate the elements of the sentence content, one with another. Content words can also be called 'open' words. The term 'open' indicates the fact that this category of words is continually being added to as new names are created and new terminology to denote actions is coined.

● **Function words:** is a category sometimes described as 'closed', indicating that this category of words tends not to be added to. As sentences are abbreviated into notes or headlines the content words form the crucial element of the abbreviation. With those words it is much easier to recover the meaning of the original text, so a note with *man bit dog* gives the reader an effective précis of the original sentence.

## Activities

A feel for the difference between these two categories of words will be of use to children developing their note-taking skills. As they undertake these activities they will be asked to look at this basic difference in the two categories of words and to use this understanding in the process of reading and recording information.

● **Photocopiable page 94 'Recreate the sentence'**
Once they have altered the sentences children can compare their revisions and look at some of the common changes made. Certain word types are commonly moved or a sentence is taken from a passive or active voice into the alternative voice.

● **Photocopiable page 95 'Join the sentence'**
This activity is like a jigsaw. Some of the strips on the left will fit several of the strips on the right, those containing the second halves of sentences. So, children need to look at all the strips and try them out before creating a full set of sentences that demonstrate agreement.

● **Photocopiable page 96 'Words that count'**
This is an oral activity for children working together in pairs trying to read the content of two passages with access to different types of words. Firstly they look at text (a), which will probably help very little. Next they hand text (a) back in and receive text (b). This is much easier to reconstruct. Having completed this they can look at the two texts together and try to read the passage.

## Further ideas

● **Headlines:** By reading items from a newspaper without their headlines, children can devise suitable headlines for news stories. If children work on the same story they can compare their headlines and see if they had any words in common.

● **Story from headline:** Looking at headlines cut from a newspaper, ask children if they can guess what the content of the story may have been. Ask them to make some brief notes on this before giving them a copy of the actual story to read.

● **Note-taking:** Record a news item from the radio (copyright permitting) and play it to a group of children, asking them to make notes as they listen. Ask them to retell the story, working round the group, contributing a fact or detail at a time. When this is complete they can listen to the original and see how close they came to recounting all the details.

## What's on the CD-ROM

On the CD-ROM you will find:
● Printable versions of all three photocopiable pages.
● Answers to 'Join the sentence'.
● Interactive version of 'Join the sentence'.

Name:

## Word order

# Recreate the sentence

■ Look at the sentences in the boxes on the left. Try to reword each of these sentences so that they say the same thing but in a different way.

■ Which words did you change? How did you change the order of the words?

| Original | New version |
|---|---|
| On Tuesday we are going to the library. | |
| My friend kicked the ball and accidentally broke the window. | |
| My friend let me use his bike to ride to school today. | |
| Tomorrow late children will stay in for the whole of playtime. | |
| After dinner we went to science club instead of going out to play. | |
| My little brother crawled into the garden and we found him eating a worm from the flower bed. | |
| There is an odd smell coming from the cellar and we have to hold our noses when we go past. | |
| I don't like custard but I like every other pudding. | |
| The green apples were bruised because they fell out of the basket. | |
| We went to the park then we had our tea. | |

## Word order

# Join the sentence

■ Match the sentence beginnings on the left-hand side of the page with the endings on the right-hand side of the page to make a set of **ten** sentences that make sense.

| | |
|---|---|
| The marbles fell out of the bag and | it is sunny. |
| Our dog ran into the house and | they rolled under the table. |
| I called for my friend and | she was not at home. |
| My sister came home and | gave it to my teacher. |
| I called for my friend but | it was raining. |
| I collected my books and | I made her a drink. |
| I found my maths book and | he rolled under the table. |
| You can come to my house and | gave them to the librarian. |
| We wanted to play outside but | we will play computer games. |
| We are going out to play and | we went to the cinema. |

Name: _____

# Word order

# Words that count

■ Read the passages below. There are words missing – can you make sense of them?

_____

**(Invention a)**

The ____ ____ was ____ in ____. ____ of ____ was ____ around ____ ____.

He ____ the ____ ____ ____. In his ____ ____ ____ ____ of ____ ____ out of a

____. These ____ ____ a ____. It was ____ as a ____.

_____

**(Invention b)**

____ steam engine ____ invented ____ Africa. Hero ____ Alexandria ____ born

____ 20CE. ____ invented ____ first steam engine. ____ ____ simple machine

two jets ____ steam spurted ____ ____ ____ container. ____ jets turned ____

sphere. ____ ____ used ____ ____ toy.

_____

**(Body a)**

____ are ____ by ____ ____ the ____ of our ____. When the ____ ____ it can

____ the ____ ____ under the ____. They ____ ____ and this ____ up as a ____

____. This is a ____. The ____ is ____ up of ____ ____ from ____ ____ and

____. If the ____ is ____ the ____ can ____ up to ____ a ____.

_____

**(Body b)**

Bruises ____ made ____ objects hitting ____ flesh ____ ____ bodies. ____ ____

object hits ____ ____ damage ____ blood vessels ____ ____ skin. ____ release

blood ____ ____ shows ____ ____ ____ purple patch. ____ ____ ____ bruise.

____ bruise ____ made ____ ____ fluid released ____ blood vessels ____ cells.

____ ____ head ____ struck ____ bruise ____ swell ____ ____ make ____ bump.

# Writing prepositions

## Objective

Use a range of prepositions to enhance precision in writing.

## Writing focus

These activities develop children's understanding of the functions of prepositions in relation to real texts they create. There is an emphasis on using factual writing, set in contexts children can either envisage or physically explore, so that the vocabulary of prepositions can be applied.

## Skills to writing

### ● When and where

Look out for the use of prepositions in texts. On locating them, look at the questions they answer about 'when' and 'where'. The first sentence in this activity's notes uses the preposition 'in', to answer the question *Where are the prepositions?* As they examine these uses, draw children's attention to the additional touch of detail that is usually provided, linked to the preposition.

### ● Preposition blanks

When reading a text to children, try presenting them with a sentence in which you say 'blank' for each preposition. They then suggest prepositions that could fill the blanks. Sometimes this involves an element of reasoning across the sentence. The first sentence in the 'Hands across the water' text on photocopiable page 87 'Preposition spaces' begins '_____ weeks…' A number of prepositions could fill that blank (for example, 'after', 'before'). A reading of the whole sentence narrows the options. When presenting children with modelled examples of writing, you can try doing this and having them suggest fillers for the gaps.

### ● Report writing

Prepositions have a particularly vital role to play in report writing. They can act as a stimulus to the writing of a report text, in which children flesh out the detail of a subject. If, for example, they are writing a leaflet

advertising an adventure playground, the various activities need placing around the location.

### ● News

Prepositions can provide a way of teasing out the details that surround a news story – particularly if children are writing a news recount about an event they were involved in. As any teacher who has had to solve a conflict can tell us, the issue of who did what when and who started it is vital. Children can use the prepositions on the poster to tease out details of their news story, expanding on the question of what happened, and where and when the various details fall.

## Activities

### ● Photocopiable page 99 'Fantasy land'

Using the map on the photocopiable sheet, children can produce a set of directions for the visitor to this fantasy land. What locations will they have to pass through, skirt around and fly over (and how will they make these journeys)? Once they have written up the text, they could try producing it in an antiquated font on parchment-like paper. This could also generate ideas for a story that includes the journey.

### ● Photocopiable page 100 'Word count'

The section on key words explores the way in which a text can be expanded or contracted with unnecessary words edited down. In this activity, children are asked to read the text and edit out extraneous material, aiming to reduce the length of the text. To set the scene for this activity, it may be worth asking children to imagine that they are newspaper editors and part of their job is to get this story to fit a 175-word space. A possible pared-down version is shown below:

> A Stanwidge puppeteer is in trouble with the authorities. Dave Kelly, whose puppet show 'Crocodella' is a favourite in Stanwidge schools, has been taken to task by the Local Education Authority. Officials say the show teaches children to misbehave. In the show, Crocodella sneaks out of school to attend a ball with Prince Croc. "This is not the sort of behaviour we want to encourage," a spokesperson for the Authority said. "Truancy is a big enough problem without children seeing it promoted in a show."
>
> Dave Kelly says he is flabbergasted by the

accusations. "It's just a bit of harmless fun," he says "and I am stunned anyone could think this show encourages children to behave like Crocodella." His pleas haven't stopped education officials writing to all primary schools suggesting they do not show the show. Mr Kelly says he is working on a new show and hopes this one will be less problematic.

## Write on

### Rosie's journey

Taking *Rosie's Walk* by Pat Hutchins (Red Fox) as their inspiration, children can devise their own story in which a character takes an interesting journey across, through and around various obstacles. They may also want to include a pursuer like Rosie's fox. This could provide stimulation for an illustrated text that children can then share with younger classes.

### Brick build

Working in pairs, children can use duplicate sets of bricks. One child has to construct a tower or structure from their bricks – as complex as possible. They then direct their partner to build the same tower, using only verbal directions (*Put the green cube next to the red cylinder*). As they do this, ask the children to listen out for the way in which instructions like this involve a large number of prepositions.

### Your route to school

Children can write out the directions of their walk to school, trying to use as many prepositions as they can. At first it may seem difficult to use a preposition like 'under' but when encouraged to incorporate it, the children will recall telephone wires or street signs 'under' which they pass.

### One moment

A number of stories are made up of the coming together of characters who have complex interactions in the past, sometimes interweaving one character's storyline with another. Good examples include *Holes* by Louis Sachar (Bloomsbury) and *The Invention of Hugo Cabret* by Brian Selznick (Scholastic Children's Books). Children could plan out their own complex story in which various

characters all come together at one particular moment – like a lift getting stuck or a group of people trapped by rising flood waters. What happened before, after and during the different events that have led each character to be here? Children could work in groups of four constructing such a scenario.

### Clues

Ask children to devise a treasure trail that could be set around school. What clues would they write? Would the next clue be on or under something? Would the next clue be taped in front or beneath something? Challenge them to use as many prepositions in their clue trail as they can.

## What's on the CD-ROM

On the CD-ROM you will find:
- Printable versions of both photocopiable pages.
- Answers to 'Word count'.

# Fantasy land

■ Plan a route around and across the map, seeing what story ideas it generates.
■ Can you find seven keys?

Illustrations © 2008, Moreno Chiacchiera/Beehive Illustration.

Name:

# Word count

■ Here is a newspaper story. It is over 300 words long. Use a pencil to cross out words that you could delete without spoiling the story. Try to reduce the story to 175 words or less.

A children's puppeteer from Stanwidge is in big trouble with some of the officials and authorities in the town. Dave Kelly, whose puppet show 'Crocodella' has for a very long, long time been a really big favourite among young children in lots of Norwich schools has recently been seriously taken to task by the officers of the Local Education Authority. Officials say they think that the show teaches young and innocent children to misbehave. In the puppet show, 'Crocodella', it would appear, sneaks out of her school to secretly and quietly attend a palace ball and to dance with another character, the nice and attractive Prince Croc. "I can tell you now clearly and without a doubt in plain words that this is not the sort of behaviour we want to encourage in the schools of the town of Stanwidge," a spokesperson for the Authority said. "We think and really are convinced that truancy is a big enough problem without children seeing it promoted in a show, that is what we say." Dave Kelly says he is completely and totally flabbergasted by the accusations made by the officers of the Local Education Authority. "My response would be to say that it's just a bit of harmless fun," he says, "and I am stunned anyone could think this show encourages children to behave like Crocodella, the puppet who is in the story that I do in the puppet show." His desperate pleas haven't stopped the education officials of the Local Education Authority writing to all of the town's primary schools and in the letter he has written suggesting they do not show the puppet show in school. Mr Kelly says that at the moment he is currently working on a brand, spanking new show and he really, really hopes that this one will prove to be less problematic.

# Chapter 5

# Long and short sentences

## Introduction

The reworking of sentences and punctuating of longer sentences forms the main focus of this chapter. As children develop their use of grammar, they develop the ability to create longer and more complex sentences. Some sections look at some of the choices writers make as they create the sentences they desire.

## In this chapter

| | |
|---|---|
| **Sentence construction** <br> page 104 | Construct sentences in different ways. |
| **Punctuation** <br> page 108 | Use punctuation in longer, more complex sentences. |
| **Embedded clauses and commas** <br> page 112 | Secure the use of the comma in embedding clauses within sentences. |
| **Punctuating complex sentences** <br> page 116 | Use punctuation marks accurately in complex sentences. |
| **Crafting sentences in writing** <br> page 120 | Apply clause structure and punctuation in writing. |

## Poster notes

### Connectives (page 102)
The poster lists various words and phrases that can act as connectives. These words play a vital role in the construction of longer and more complex sentences. The poster will be of particular use in 'Sentence construction'.

### Punctuation notes (page 103)
The poster shows the various punctuation marks performing their function. It can provide a discussion point as children find the various marks in their relevant sentences and look at the function they are performing, for example, what is being tagged on by the dash.

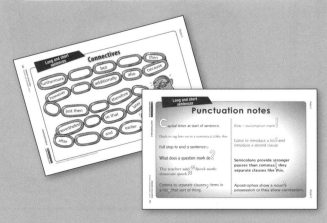

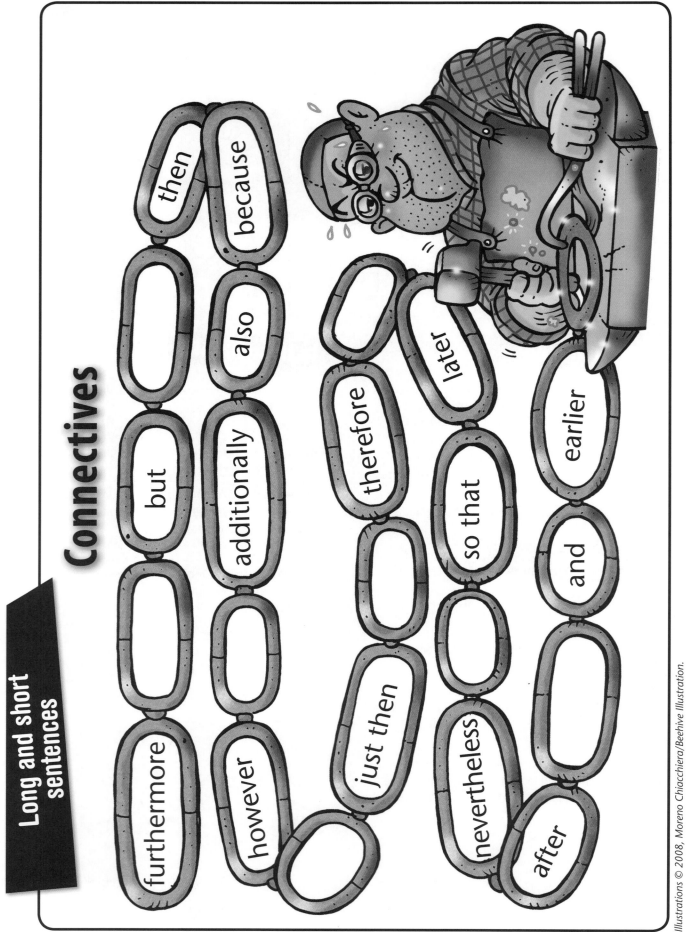

# Connectives

**Long and short sentences**

then

because

but

also

additionally

furthermore

however

just then

therefore

later

so that

earlier

and

nevertheless

after

# Punctuation notes

**Long and short sentences**

Capital letter at start of sentence.

Dash to tag bits on to a sentence☐like this.

Full stop to end a sentence○

What does a question mark do○?

The teacher said 66*Speech marks demarcate speech.*99

Comma to separate clauses, items in a list, that sort of thing.

Wow – *exclamation mark* ○

Colon to introduce a list○ and introduce a second clause.

**Semicolons provide stronger pauses than commas; they separate clauses like this.**

Apostrophes show a noun's possession or they show contraction.

# Sentence construction

## Objective

Construct sentences in different ways.

## Background knowledge

Anyone who has agonised over writing a letter knows that there are numerous ways of saying the same thing. The varied ways of putting something into words may change the meaning of a sentence slightly, and the language can sound harsher or more flowery. Sentences can be extended by adding more words or can have words deleted from them. They can also be rearranged, or completely different ways can be found for saying the same thing.

## Activities

As children experience the varied ways in which sentences can be altered, one important aspect of this work is to encourage them to consider how they phrase the sentences they use in their day-to-day written work. An understanding of this aspect of grammar is what proficient writers use when they pause to consider the best way to say something.

● **Photocopiable page 105 'Two sentences into one'**
Once children have remodelled their sentences, they can compare the changes they made. The various uses of connectives can be interesting.

● **Photocopiable page 106 'Contract the sentence'**
The aim in this activity is to reduce each sentence to ten words or less. They are all sentences containing a fairly large degree of information. One tactic here is for children to look at the words that carry the essential content of the sentence, circle these and see how they can then model them into a clear sentence.

● **Photocopiable page 107 'Two for one'**
Children who have completed the matching activity might also be able to offer opinions on which version of each sentence they feel is preferable.

## Further ideas

● **Short news:** Children can look through a selection of newspapers to find the shortest news stories and look at how much information has been put into that number of words.
● **Cut stories:** Another activity looking at news stories involves children reading newspaper stories and seeing if they can find words that could be cut. It is not an easy task, as journalism tends to involve a tight word count but it provides scope for the budding editors in the class.
● **Reword a paragraph:** Taking a paragraph from a book, children can try to remodel it completely. This may involve the addition, removal or exchange of words or the complete rewriting of certain sentences.

##  What's on the CD-ROM

On the CD-ROM you will find:
● Printable versions of all three photocopiable pages.
● Answers to all three photocopiable pages.
● Interactive version of 'Two for one'.

**Sentence construction**

# Two sentences into one

You can take two short sentences:

| It was raining. | Playtime was indoors. |

and turn them into one, for example:

| It was raining so playtime was indoors. |

or:

| Playtime was indoors because it was raining. |

■ Try turning these sets of two sentences into one complex sentence.

| Jan's clothes were wet. | He fell in the pond. |

| |

| My shoes were dirty. | I cleaned them. |

| |

| The water boiled. | Gran made a cup of tea. |

| |

| Mum dropped the mug. | It broke. |

| |

| Our tortoise is hibernating. | We will bring it indoors. |

| |

**SCHOLASTIC** **PHOTOCOPIABLE**
www.scholastic.co.uk
Scholastic Literacy Skills
Grammar and punctuation: Year 5 **105**

Name:

**Sentence construction**

# Contract the sentence

■ Look at the sentences. Try to contract them into smaller sentences. Try making contracted sentences of **ten** words or fewer.

The girls found the lost boy in the shop and took him to the security guard.

*Girls take lost boy to security guard.*

_____

Naima fell off the swing, broke her arm and had to go to hospital.

_____

Mr Cole, who owns the corner shop, won £1,000 in a crossword competition.

_____

The lever came off the drinks fountain and flooded the school corridor.

_____

Ms Holder lost her voice and couldn't teach the choir so they practised by themselves.

_____

A taxi skidded off the road and knocked down the side wall of the playground.

_____

The builders' scaffolding collapsed and lots of different colours of paint spattered across the wall they were painting.

_____

The local cinema has had to close down because it is infested with rats.

_____

**Sentence construction**

# Two for one

■ The sentences below make sets of two. Each set consists of two sentences referring to the same thing. Can you match them up?

| | |
|---|---|
| We can't go out to play because of the rain. | Loads of conkers fell out of the tree because of the ball being thrown. |
| Ms Kahn is ill today so Ms Porter will be teaching us. | The children were excellent during the fire practice. |
| James threw the ball into the tree and a load of conkers fell to the ground. | Our teacher will, today, be replaced by another teacher. |
| There was a fire drill at school and the children were brilliant. | The rain is preventing us from playing out. |

■ Make your own sentences in pairs, saying the same thing in different ways.

Illustrations © 2008, Moreno Chiacchiera/Beehive Illustration.

# Punctuation

### Objective

Use punctuation in longer, more complex sentences.

### Background knowledge

Complex sentences are made up of more than one distinct section. Each section is called a 'clause'. If a sentence states *The cat sat on the mat*, it gives a simple verbal description of where the cat performed the act of sitting. A more complex sentence might be: *Before eating its owner, the cat sat on the mat, scratching it to shreds with those razor-like claws.* More information has been imported into this sentence: information concerning the nature of the cat, what it did to the mat and what activity preceded this action.

● **Main clauses:** are the essential part of a sentence (The cat sat on the mat'). Main clauses are able to stand independently, so 'The cat sat on the mat' makes sense by itself.

● **Subordinate clauses:** are the ones that are tagged on in order to supply further information ('Before eating its owner', 'scratching it…' and so on) A subordinate clause like 'Before eating its owner' only makes sense when tagged on to a main clause.

### Activities

The addition of clauses increases the complexity of sentences, so increasing the level of punctuation required. Simple sentences often make sense merely with a capital letter and a full stop. Add speech, raise a question or insert a clause – each of these changes requires the addition of punctuation marks.

● **Photocopiable page 109 'Punctuation checklist'**
The checklist provides an opportunity for children to look at a range of texts they have shared in the classroom, finding examples of the main points of punctuation and reflecting on their use, based on the context in which they encounter them.

● **Photocopiable page 110 'Sentences to redraft'**
The unpunctuated sentences provide an opportunity for utilising a range of punctuation marks.

● **Photocopiable page 111 'Tricks page'**
As they find examples of the various punctuation marks in use, children can try to ensure they link all of the pieces of punctuation in this text with one of the marks at the edge.

### Further ideas

● **Punctuating challenge:** Children can try creating a single sentence that contains the maximum number of punctuation marks they can squeeze into it.

● **Poster:** Using the checklist from photocopiable page 109 'Punctuation checklist' as a guide, children can try to create a poster that teaches the various punctuation points. They can include definitions of the different marks and examples of their usage.

### What's on the CD-ROM

On the CD-ROM you will find:
● Printable versions of all three photocopiable pages.
● Answers to 'Sentences to redraft'.
● Interactive version of 'Sentences to redraft'.

## Punctuation

# Punctuation checklist

■ Read sections from a text. Look for the following pieces of punctuation, ticking each one you find. Can you explain the jobs they do?

■ The question mark box is completed as an example.

? – " " ! , : ' ; A ·

| Punctuation mark | ✔ | Function (the job it does) |
|---|---|---|
| Question mark | ✔ | Shows that a sentence is a question. |
| Capital letter | | |
| Full stop | | |
| Speech marks | | |
| Comma | | |
| Exclamation mark | | |
| Colon | | |
| Dash | | |
| Apostrophe | | |
| Semicolon | | |

Name:

## Punctuation

# Sentences to redraft

■ Rewrite these sentences, inserting the punctuation that they need in order to make sense.

are we doing art today _____

jordan said I am going to spain for my holidays and I said great I wish I could go

_____

_____

to make pancakes you need eggs butter flour and milk

_____

on Tuesday the day after tomorrow it is lornas birthday and weve been invited to her party

_____

_____

find these parts on the bicycle diagram the handlebars brakes saddle and wheels

_____

_____

stop the children shouted but the bus driver who was singing to himself hadnt heard the bell

_____

_____

can you finish your work please the teacher asked the children playtime has started

_____

_____

sam my uncle is starting work today at my granddads cafe

_____

dont run in the corridor mr carter shouted as the children rushed out of the room

_____

_____

## Punctuation

# Tricks page

■ Look at this comic page and try to find the pieces of punctuation illustrated around the border. Draw a line connecting each punctuation point to an example in the text.

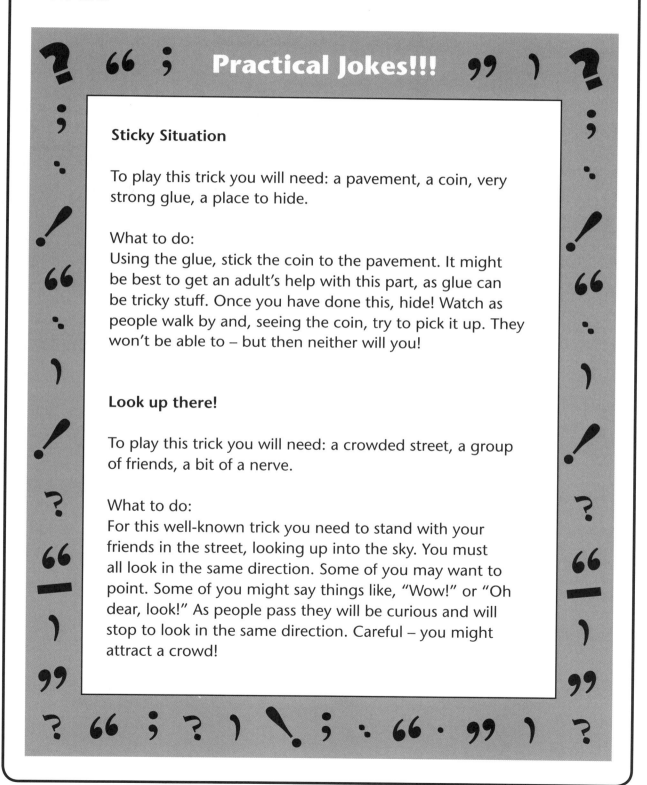

**Practical Jokes!!!**

**Sticky Situation**

To play this trick you will need: a pavement, a coin, very strong glue, a place to hide.

What to do:
Using the glue, stick the coin to the pavement. It might be best to get an adult's help with this part, as glue can be tricky stuff. Once you have done this, hide! Watch as people walk by and, seeing the coin, try to pick it up. They won't be able to – but then neither will you!

**Look up there!**

To play this trick you will need: a crowded street, a group of friends, a bit of a nerve.

What to do:
For this well-known trick you need to stand with your friends in the street, looking up into the sky. You must all look in the same direction. Some of you may want to point. Some of you might say things like, "Wow!" or "Oh dear, look!" As people pass they will be curious and will stop to look in the same direction. Careful – you might attract a crowd!

# Embedded clauses and commas

## Objective

Secure the use of the comma in embedding clauses within sentences.

## Background knowledge

Clauses can be embedded within sentences, providing additional information on the subject of the main clause. In the sentence *The dog, who had caught a bad dose of fleas, scratched and scratched*, the embedded clause 'who had caught a bad dose of fleas' provides additional information about the dog. Such clauses are demarcated with commas. Care needs to be taken. An 'embedded clause' is one that can be removed, leaving a sentence that makes sense. In the above example, the removal of the embedded clause leaves one in which the sense of the dog still scratching is retained.

In the sentence *Dogs who catch fleas need powder* the words 'who catch fleas' do not constitute an embedded clause. They are part of a larger noun phrase 'Dogs who catch fleas'. The sentence is not referring to all dogs, just to a specific category (those who catch fleas).

## Activities

The emphasis in these activities is upon the way in which embedded clauses can be placed within a sentence. They can also be removed without any loss of sense. The activities encourage children to look at examples of the ways in which this occurs by remodelling various complex sentences.

● **Photocopiable page 113 'Embedded clauses'**
This activity both explains and investigates the use of embedded clauses.

● **Photocopiable page 114 'Embedding the clause'**
In this activity children take a clause and locate the point at which they would embed it within a sentence.

● **Photocopiable page 115 'Clause matching'**
Part of the process of understanding when and how to place embedded clauses within a sentence involves knowing the type of clause that is demarcated in this way. This activity explores the type of clause that will be placed in specific sentences.

## Further ideas

● **Clause snatching:** Children can look at long and complex sentences from stories. They can write these on a whiteboard or sheet of paper. They can look at the clauses they can remove that leave the sentence intact.
● **Redrafting:** Ask children to look at their own writing and to record extracts that could have been presented as sentences with embedded clauses. Can they rewrite their sentences in this way?

##  What's on the CD-ROM

On the CD-ROM you will find:
● Printable versions of all three photocopiable pages.
● Answers to all three photocopiable pages.
● Interactive versions of 'Embedded clauses' and 'Clause matching'.

**Embedded clauses
and commas**

# Embedded clauses

These sentences each contain a middle section that adds something to the main clause of the sentence.
So, in the sentence:

> The dog, who had caught a bad dose of fleas, scratched and scratched.

the section between commas tells us something about the dog and could be removed, leaving a sentence that makes sense.
The sections in the middle are called embedded clauses and should be marked out with commas.

■ Look at these sentences. Which words are embedded clauses? Shade over them in colouring pencil, and put commas either side of them.

My sister who starts Brownies today has new shoes.

The green door which has no window needs repairing.

My mum realising she had no bus fare had to go back home.

Last night the school caretaker who lives in a house beside the school had to repair two broken windows.

On Tuesday after school has finished I am going swimming.

The chocolate cake which my mum had hidden had been eaten up.

My friend the one that lives in Scotland is coming to stay for a holiday.

After school if it isn't raining we are going for a picnic.

My brother without thinking about it jumped off the top diving board.

Today my bicycle which hasn't worked for weeks is going to the repair shop.

Name:

**Embedded clauses and commas**

# Embedding the clause

■ Look at these sentences. They each have a strip that can be embedded somewhere in the middle of the sentence.

| The dog, | who had caught a bad dose of fleas, | scratched and scratched. |

■ Cut the strips out and stick them on a sheet of paper. Place the embedded clauses in the sentences. Mark them out with commas.

| | | |
|---|---|---|
| My great grandmother | rides a motorbike. | who comes from Cornwall |
| My house | needs lots of repairs. | which is very old |
| You are | a great class. | I can honestly say |
| My mum | is going to have a big party. | when she celebrates her birthday |
| Our football team | is the best in our area. | having won the cup |
| My dad | comes home at weekends. | who works in London |
| Astronauts | eat food from tubes. | while out in space |
| Our cat | needs a bath. | who happens to smell |

**Embedded clauses and commas**

# Clause matching

■ These clauses fit into the sentences below.

the one with the puncture
my mum's sister
the green one
my mother's mother
the new one
the one with the bandaged paw
the big old building
the one in the village

■ Try to put the right clause in the right sentence.

My dog, _____, needs to see a vet.

My Gran, _____, has got false teeth.

Our school, _____, is getting knocked down.

My sister's bike, _____, needs repairing.

Today the computer, _____, broke down.

Aunty Lou, _____, is visiting us.

The old oak tree, _____, blew down in the storm.

My toothbrush, _____, has lost its bristles.

Illustrations © 2008, Moreno Chiacchiera/Beehive Illustration.

# Punctuating complex sentences

## Objective

Use punctuation marks accurately in complex sentences.

## Background knowledge

These activities revise some of the main points of punctuation which children should be developing an understanding of, notably:

- **capital letter:** at the start of a sentence
- **full stop:** to end a sentence
- **question mark:** to denote a question
- **speech marks:** to demarcate speech
- **comma:** to separate clauses and items in a list
- **exclamation mark:** to show an exclamation
- **colon:** to introduce a list or to introduce a second clause
- **semicolon:** to provide a stronger pause than a comma, separating clauses
- **apostrophe:** to show possession or contraction
- **dash:** to tag clauses onto a sentence or to use around a parenthetical clause.

## Activities

These activities provide opportunities for children to revisit the punctuation and construction of complex sentences.

- **Photocopiable page 117 'Sentence looping'**
The correct use of punctuation involves being familiar with certain aspects of sentences. In this activity children use colouring pencils to demarcate some of the significant aspects of sentences that are punctuated in particular ways. Their looping of speech develops awareness of where they should place speech marks. The looping of clauses develops an understanding of where they should place clause-separating items of punctuation such as commas and colons. Awareness of questions develops use of the question mark.

- **Photocopiable page 118 'Punctuation hunt'**
As they look for examples of punctuation children should develop their understanding of the actual uses of the various types of punctuation revised here.
- **Photocopiable page 119 'In this sentence…'**
The lists to the side of the sentences in this activity give children a clear idea of the punctuation they can insert into the sentences.

## Further ideas

- **Revision:** Children can try to make up their own examples of how each of the punctuation marks covered would be put to use.
- **Revisiting writing:** Children can look back at their writing over the course of the school year and look at how their use of punctuation has developed.

 ## What's on the CD-ROM

On the CD-ROM you will find:
- Printable versions of all three photocopiable pages.
- Answers to 'Sentence looping' and 'In this sentence…'.
- Interactive versions of 'Sentence looping' and 'In this sentence…'.

**Punctuating complex sentences**

# Sentence looping

■ Look at the unpunctuated sentences below and circle different bits in different colours.
- Circle words that are spoken in red.
- Circle sub-clauses in green.
- Circle sentences that are questions in blue.

louise said help me do this jigsaw

is it time for dinner

on Tuesday after school finishes we go to club

lola said lets go ice skating next friday

the teacher said its time for our spelling test

after thinking for a while sam said lets go to my house

we went to blackpool which was a big treat

can you play a cd on this player

our class decided after a lot of thinking to have a party

*Illustrations © 2008, Moreno Chiacchiera/Beehive Illustration.*

Name:

**Punctuating complex sentences**

# Punctuation hunt

■ Look through newspapers, leaflets and magazines and try to find examples of the following pieces of punctuation. Cut them out and stick them in the table.

| | |
|---|---|
| full stop | |
| question mark | |
| speech marks | |
| comma | |
| exclamation mark | |
| colon | |
| hyphen | |
| semicolon | |
| apostrophe | |
| dash | |

Illustrations © 2008, Moreno Chiacchiera/Beehive Illustration.

**PHOTOCOPIABLE**  ■SCHOLASTIC
www.scholastic.co.uk

## Punctuating complex sentences

# In this sentence...

■ Each of these sentences could be rewritten to contain the types of punctuation shown in the list alongside.

■ Rewrite the sentences, adding the punctuation shown in the lists.

sara shouted at the top of her voice i won i won

_____

_____

| speech marks |
| --- |
| exclamation mark |
| three capital letters |
| two commas |

the room was painted in many colours blue green bright pink and yellow

_____

_____

| capital letter |
| --- |
| colon |
| two commas |
| full stop |

sallys coat is lost does anyone know where it is

_____

_____

| capital letter |
| --- |
| apostrophe |
| dash |
| question mark |

the fifth of may my birthday is only three days away

_____

_____

| two capital letters |
| --- |
| full stop |
| two commas |

as the alligator which had escaped from the zoo slipped into the classroom the children shouted help help

_____

_____

| three capital letters |
| --- |
| two exclamation marks |
| four commas |
| speech marks |

jacks worst nightmare came true when the teacher asked can you sing a solo in assembly

_____

_____

| two capital letters |
| --- |
| apostrophe |
| question mark |
| speech marks |
| comma |

# Crafting sentences in writing

## Objective

Apply clause structure and punctuation in writing.

## Writing focus

In this chapter, the focus has been on redrafting sentences with a view towards both punctuating them fully and accurately, and ensuring children develop their use of clause structure. Both these features come to the fore when they are applied to the children's current writing. Many of these activities involve reflection on writing already done, rather than the creation of new pieces.

## Skills to writing

● **Sentence crafting**

One of the key features of this chapter has been that the same sentence could be written in different ways. The skilled writer will stop and reflect on alternative wording that could be used for expressiveness and precision. Encourage children to think about the different ways in which one idea can be translated into more than one sentence, like on photocopiable page 107 'Two for one'. Encourage them to come up with, and note down, examples, sharing them with the class and discussing which option is preferred. Can they find three options?

● **Two sentences or one**

Look out for the times when two short sentences could be come one extended sentence – as on photocopiable page 105 'Two sentences into one'. There are times when the two short sentences will be more appropriate. Sometimes these are better. They can have a particular effect. At other times one longer sentence may be preferred. So, the previous sentences in this text could have read: *Sometimes these are better and they can have a particular effect*. Ask children to look for 'two to one' possibilities in their own writing.

● **Cut and embed**

Using the ideas from 'Embedded clauses and commas' (see page 112), ask children to look for sentences in their own writing, where they could write the original on a strip of paper, and then see a point where they could cut the sentence and embed a clause. If they have written *Yesterday we went to the pantomime*, should they write *Yesterday, because we had been such a great class, we went to the pantomime*?

● **Colour coding**

As children reflect on their writing, they may be able to use the sort of colour coding that was used on photocopiable page 117 'Sentence looping'. When editing previous pieces of writing, ask them to look for at least two features they can either highlight as included or that could have been used. They can use different colours for these – so speech punctuation can be ticked in green and use of question marks in red. One of the main functions performed here is to send children back to their work, looking for more than one feature of punctuation or grammar. The colours provide a guide in such twin-tracked activities.

## Activities

● **Photocopiable page 122 'Sentence pairs'**

Using the examples of photocopiable page 107 'Two for one', children can devise their own examples of two simple and shorter sentences that could be joined together to create a longer sentence. It's best if they can gather the shorter examples from their own writing, as this develops that whole idea of reflecting on our sentence construction with a view towards extending it.

● **Photocopiable page 123 'My punctuation'**

This page provides a framework for children to collect their own uses of some of the varied punctuation marks covered up to this point. It does involve a fair bit of copying, as the idea is that children should look through their writing to find real and uncontrived examples of their personal use of these various punctuation marks. The examples they find should be copied and put in the spaces shown on the chart. As children collect a range of different punctuation marks, the task provides a visible way of celebrating their progress in this aspect of the craft of writing.

## Write on

● **Excuses**

This morning everyone was late for school. Using the connectives on poster page 102, ask the children to write excuses that are elaborate and imaginative – and impress the angry teacher by using the full range of connectives. On the way to school something happened, and then something else, and just then… and after that…. Once they have written up these paragraphs of imaginative tales, children can practise saying them to a po-faced teacher. For inspiration, try reading Jill Murphy's *On the Way Home* (Macmillian Children's Books), a classic of tall-story making.

● **Details**

Using the idea of the embedded clause, children can revisit writing they have done, seeing where they could embed a clause that adds an extra bit of detail. If, in a story about being late, they wrote *My teacher was very angry*, they could embed a clause that says something about the character – maybe a detail about his attitude to lateness or her appearance that morning (*My teacher who had turned a tomato shade of temper, was very angry*). Children can be guided to see embedded clauses as a way of adding an element of fun to their writing.

● **Speech punctuation**

Speech can provide a good focus for developing children's use of punctuation. As they imagine characters in a narrative, or develop speech in a recount, ask them to look at the way certain punctuation marks can stimulate their writing.

In the course of writing a conversation:

● Could one character ask another a question?

● Will a character make a sudden exclamation – and if so, why?

● As a character says one thing, could they add a bit of extra detail (punctuated by placing a comma where it is needed)?

● When giving a bit of extra detail, could one character make a short digression, embedded in a clause?

The aim here is not to see punctuation as a forced inclusion, but rather to use it as a stimulus to suggest to a writer ways of developing a piece of writing.

## What's on the CD-ROM

On the CD-ROM you will find:
● Printable versions of both photocopiable pages.

Name:

**Crafting sentences in writing**

# Sentence pairs

■ Can you write examples of two sentences that say the same thing? The first one has been done for you.

| | |
|---|---|
| We can't go out to play because of the rain. | The rain is preventing us from playing out. |
| | |
| | |
| | |

**Crafting sentences in writing**

# My punctuation

■ Look through your writing and find examples of different punctuation marks you have used. Jot down the sentences in which you used them. If you've not used that many – you can collect them here when you do!

| Punctuation mark | My sentence |
|---|---|
|  |  |
|  |  |
|  |  |
|  |  |
|  |  |
|  |  |
|  |  |
|  |  |
|  |  |
|  |  |

# Chapter 6

# Sentences and readers

## Introduction

This chapter looks at various factors that feature in the way sentences are presented for readers. These include considerations such as the various methods a writer can use to present speech and the significance of word order. As children undertake these sections they should take the opportunity to reflect upon their own writing, particularly of texts that recount events, and consider the way they aim their writing at a reader.

## In this chapter

| | |
|---|---|
| **Speech and writing** page 127 | Investigate the difference between spoken and written language. |
| **Direct and reported speech** page 131 | Understand the difference between direct and reported speech. |
| **Reader guides** page 135 | Understand the ways in which punctuation and the setting out of dialogue aid the reader. |
| **Audiences and sentences** page 139 | Review and edit sentences with reference to the audience of a text. |
| **Writing speech** page 143 | Accurately and imaginatively present speech in writing. |

## Poster notes

### Ways of showing speech (page 125)

The four most common ways in which texts represent speech are shown on this poster. The two most common ones in narrative text are direct speech and reported speech.

### Ways of saying (page 126)

This poster provides a place to record particular ways of saying. You may decide to collect ways of saying 'good', in which case this will be written in the centre. Children can then suggest various standard and non-standard ways of saying something is good, such as 'brill' and 'wicked'. Other 'ways of saying' can be tried, ideas for which can be drawn from photocopiable page 129 'Ways of saying'.

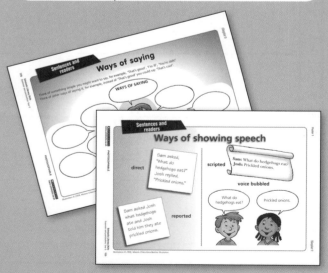

# Ways of showing speech

**scripted**

Sam: What do hedgehogs eat?
Josh: Prickled onions.

**voice bubbled**

Prickled onions.

What do hedgehogs eat?

**direct**

Sam asked, "What do hedgehogs eat?" Josh replied, "Prickled onions."

**reported**

Sam asked Josh what hedgehogs ate and Josh told him they ate prickled onions.

# Ways of saying

Think of something simple you might want to say, for example, 'That's good', 'I'm ill', 'You're daft!'
Think of other ways of saying it, for example, instead of 'That's good' you could say 'That's cool'.

WAYS OF SAYING

Illustrations © 2008, Moreno Chiacchiera/Beehive Illustration.

# Speech and writing

## Objective

Investigate the difference between spoken and written language.

## Background knowledge

Speech and writing form two different modes of communication. Speech is usually rooted in a context in which the communicator can point or in which the items referred to are obvious. The speaker can also use facial expressions, so a speaker can say *It was lovely* while grimacing to indicate irony in their words. Writing is uprooted from its context. Standing in a car repair shop someone asking a person in overalls 'Have you finished with it?' is likely to be asking about the fate of his or her car. Out of that context the written sentence *Have you finished with it?* remains open.

In speech a communicator can pause, use inflections of the voice, and so on; in writing such prosody is communicated through punctuation. In speech sentences can be varied. Speech can be broken up and not necessarily in complete sentences; in writing the norm is the formation of complete sentences.

## Activities

As children's writing develops, so does their grasp of the conventions associated with this mode. Younger children will often write in a way that does not account for the need to communicate out of context. They will often write exactly as they speak. Here the differences between speech and writing are explored, with the intention of raising children's awareness of the conventions that the written mode places on communication.

● **Photocopiable page 128 'Transcripts'**
This activity provides two examples of text including the sorts of breaks and flows of speech that characterise the spoken mode. The unpunctuated and staccato nature of these texts should contrast with the written sentences that the children produce.

● **Photocopiable page 129 'Ways of saying'**
Part of the standardisation of English is the way in which certain words and phrases develop an acceptability. By investigating the different ways in which certain things can and have been said in the (not too distant) past children encounter the changes in expression over time.

● **Photocopiable page 130 'Speech and writing'**
The obvious difference between the speech and writing in this activity is the number of words in the sentences. Once they have completed this activity, children can investigate the way in which the pronouns in the spoken form need clarification when taken out of an immediate context and put into writing.

## Further ideas

● **List the differences:** Children can draw up a list of the differences between speech and writing, comparing the two modes.

● **Borge's punctuation:** The comedian Victor Borge had an act in which he ascribed a different sound (such as a popping noise or raspberry) to each punctuation mark. Children can work in groups devising their own examples and apply these to selected sentences.

● **Tape adults:** Children could ask for permission to tape-record willing adults around the school doing things like lining up their class and supervising dinner time. They could use the tapes to locate sections of speech and listen for the way these sound compared to how the same things would be communicated in writing.

## What's on the CD-ROM

On the CD-ROM you will find:
● Printable versions of all three photocopiable pages.
● Answers to 'Transcripts' and 'Speech and writing'.
● Interactive version of 'Speech and writing'.

Name:

## Speech and writing

# Transcripts

- ■ These transcripts show exactly what two people said when they were:
  - asking for something
  - recounting an event.

- ■ How would they have looked if they were written?
- ■ Put each of them into written English and check the differences.

Oh Sara listen…listen… tell you what I was thinking, like d'ya think it'd be ok for us to do our story on your computer cos mines all bust and my mum says it ain't gonna get fixed until after pay day and its sort of awkward cos we gotta get this thing done, yeh?

Miss, miss, let me tell you about Saturday cos me and Carlos we found this bubble wrap and really big bubbles it was — all of it so we took us shoes and socks off and we walked all over it and, like, dug our heels in and pop pop pop it was like fireworks and then we started jumping on it and it was a real laugh.

## Speech and writing

# Ways of saying

New ways of expressing things are entering English all the time. During the 1970s young people described something that was good in new ways.

■ Can you think of some diverse ways in which you and your friends describe the following?

| Something is good or brilliant | Feeling ill or sick |
|---|---|
|  | 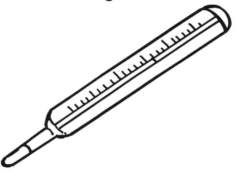 |
| Feeling miserable | Something is bad or just not very good |
|  |  |

*Illustrations © 2008, Moreno Chiacchiera/Beehive Illustration.*

Name:

# Speech and writing

# Speech and writing

■ The boxes below show a spoken way and written way of saying the same thing. The spoken way is hard to understand. For example, when someone says 'What's this?' you need to be looking at them to see what they are pointing at.
■ Can you match the spoken and written words that perform the same job?

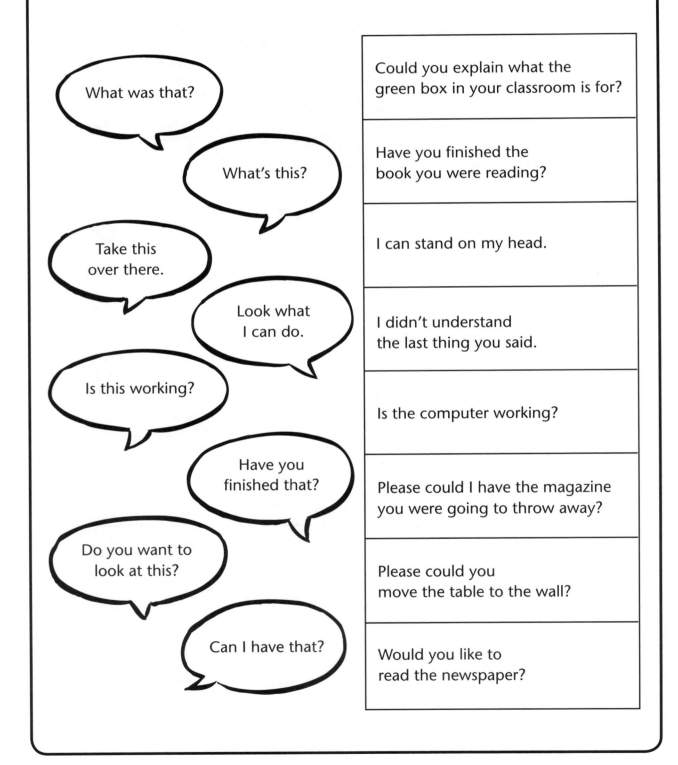

**PHOTOCOPIABLE**      ▪SCHOLASTIC
www.scholastic.co.uk

# Direct and reported speech

## Objective

Understand the difference between direct and reported speech.

## Background knowledge

The words of others can be represented in various ways in writing. This can range from a transcript, recording the speech verbatim, to a summary of what someone said in a speech. The lengthiest of speeches can be condensed into a one-sentence summary.

One significant difference is between the direct quotation of speech, with the corresponding use of speech marks, and the reporting of speech in a way that gives the idea or gist of what was said, but does not quote the actual words. So we can directly quote someone: *Victoria said 'We are not amused.'* Or indirectly report it: *Victoria said she was not amused.* Reporting can involve an element of summing up what was said: *Victoria expressed displeasure.*

## Activities

The crucial difference between direct and reported speech lies in whether or not the words on the page are presented as a quotation of what was said. These activities should provide an opportunity to revise work on speech marks and the way in which they guide readers, as well as investigating these two ways of presenting what was said.

● **Photocopiable page 132 'Direct and reported'**
Looking at the two sets of boxes, children can try to match direct with reported representations of the same pieces of speech. Some of the speech acts are remarkably similar, so children will need to check carefully to ensure that they have matched the right rectangles together.

● **Photocopiable page 133 'Who said what?'**
Through completing the speech bubbles, children will be turning reported speech into the words that could have been said. They can use their own judgement on the exact wording. When the text says *I agreed* the narrator could have a voice bubble containing the words *I agree* or *You're right* – or even plain *Yeah!*

● **Photocopiable page 134 'Change the style'**
As with the above activity, children may need to use creative judgement to decide what actual words might have been used in producing the speech acts reported.

## Further ideas

● **Finding:** Children can look through different types of text that contain speech in order to find which contain reported and direct speech. Interesting examples could include history books that narrate the events of a particular time, modern novels and different levels of a reading scheme.

● **Comic contexts:** Taking the conversation that takes place in a comic story as their starting point, children can look at how much of a comic story is dependent upon the pictures. They can try recording the dialogue from some of the pictures separately and see how much sense it makes standing alone. They could then look in the comic story and see what the context of the picture contributed to the speech.

● **Plays and pictures:** Using a scripted text, such as a playscript, children can try turning this format into a comic story. They will need to account for who said what to whom, and should draw the characters with their speech bubbles.

### What's on the CD-ROM

On the CD-ROM you will find:
● Printable versions of all three photocopiable pages.
● Answers to 'Direct and reported' and 'Change the style'.
● Interactive version of 'Direct and reported'.

Name:

# Direct and reported

Speech can be presented in two ways:

| directly, as direct quotation in speech marks giving the words that were said, for example:<br><br>Mum said, "Take those muddy boots off."<br>I said, "It's not fair." | indirectly, as reported speech not in speech marks stating what was said, for example:<br><br>Mum told us to take our muddy boots off.<br>I said it wasn't fair. |
|---|---|

■ Look at the boxes below. Sort the boxes containing direct speech from ones containing reported speech. Try matching the direct-speech boxes with the reported-speech boxes which say the same thing.

| | |
|---|---|
| I pleaded with the dragon not to eat me. | Our teacher said "Open that window." |
| I called to Jack to throw the ball to me. | Our teacher asked us to open a particular window. |
| I pleaded "Please don't eat me" with the dragon | Our teacher said we could open any window. |
| Our teacher said "Open any window you like." | "Jack," I shouted, "Throw the ball to me." |
| Mum asked "Where's the hammer?" | The dragon said "I plan to eat you." |
| The dragon said it had plans to eat me. | Mum asked where the hammer was. |
| "Don't whisper in assembly," the teacher told the children. | The teacher told the children not to whisper in assembly. |

# Who said what?

■ Look at the comic story. The bubbles are blank. Can you fill in the bubbles with your suggestions as to what each character might have said?

Our teacher said it was raining so we had to stay inside. We all moaned about how much we hated staying in.

We got all the games out. Lisa pointed out most of them were broken. I agreed.

Just then Saleh looked out the window and said the sun was coming out. We all cheered.

We all went to the window. It was still raining. Saleh said he had been joking. We told him it wasn't funny.

Illustrations © 2008, Moreno Chiacchiera/Beehive Illustration.

**Direct and reported speech**

# Change the style

■  Look at the left-hand column. Rewrite the sentences in the right-hand column. Change reported speech to direct speech and direct speech to reported speech.

| Original text | Rewritten text |
| --- | --- |
| Mum said she was making chips for tea so I told her they were my favourite. | |
| I asked, "Can we go swimming?" "The pool is closed today", Dad replied. | |
| The cyclist warned everyone to get out of the way because his brakes were not working. | |
| The teacher said, "Sit down and answer your names on the register," then he added, "Where is the register?" | |
| I asked if I could type my story on the computer and my teacher agreed. | |
| "I'll be ninety on Saturday," my gran whispered. "She's doing a parachute jump to celebrate," my mum added. | |
| My friend, Amy, told us she was moving house and we said we didn't want her to go. | |
| "I'm cold," the boy said. "Well, run up and down the stairs to warm up a bit," his mum responded. | |
| Reuben told the lifeguard he had seen a boat in trouble so the lifeguard said he would see for himself. | |

# Reader guides

## Objective

Understand the ways in which punctuation and the setting out of dialogue aid the reader.

## Background knowledge

In spoken language there are all sorts of stresses and pauses a speaker can use in order to assist the listener's understanding. One example of this is the slight pitch change people make just after saying *So I said…* to indicate that the words that follow are the actual words said on a previous occasion now quoted. In written English this is done through a variety of means. Punctuation marks can indicate the barriers between what is and is not quoted very effectively, as well as the items in a list and the completion of a sentence.

## Activities

As children develop an appreciation of the role performed by punctuation, their ability to use it in writing is enhanced. They know why a particular mark is useful so they use it. In these activities children should begin to discuss the usefulness of particular punctuation points and the role they play in assisting the reader.

● **Photocopiable page 136 'Helping the reader'**
This tightly written piece of dialogue is one example of Philip Ridley's excellent presentation of speech in his novels. Children should locate speech marks, commas, capital letters, exclamation marks, question marks, an ellipsis (three dots showing pauses) and full stops. Then ask them to analyse the role some of these marks are playing in assisting the reading of the passage.

● **Photocopiable page 137 'Unhelpful sentences'**
The puzzling read these sentences present is an important part of the exercise. By working out what is being said, children can also investigate the ways in which punctuation would ordinarily help them to read the sentences.

● **Photocopiable page 138 'Pick an argument'**
Children need to work on this in groups of six or fewer. They cut out the slips of paper and these are placed face downwards in the middle of the group. Give them a set time, around ten minutes, to write one of the arguments shown on the slips using lots of speech, clearly demarcated. Once this is clear, everyone picks a slip and has to start writing. After ten minutes everyone changes their slips around and tries to do the same with the new argument.

## Further ideas

● **Punctuation history:** If children have access to pieces of writing they did in the past, either from record folders or by bringing samples in from home, they can trace their own punctuation history. This involves looking at how they learned to use certain marks at certain times and how this has improved their writing.
● **Particular punctuation:** Ask the children to review the punctuation marks that they use with confidence and those that they still need to learn. They can decide which ones they plan to perfect over the coming weeks.
● **Page scanning:** Children can try to scan pages of text briefly and then recall what punctuation marks they saw on the page to a friend, who then checks their recollection by looking at the text.

## What's on the CD-ROM

On the CD-ROM you will find:
● Printable versions of all three photocopiable pages.
● Answers to 'Unhelpful sentences'.

## Reader guides

# Helping the reader

■ Look at this passage from *Kasper and the Glitter*. It is the scene in which Kasper has entered the city called 'The Gloom' and has met Jingo. Find the different pieces of layout and punctuation that help the reader. Note these down in the margins.

'This way, if you please, Master Kasper,' said Jingo.
He led Kasper into a long and gloomy alleyway.

Their footsteps echoed all round them.

Now that Jingo didn't have the basket to carry, he wasn't quite sure what to do with his hands. To keep them occupied, he picked up his dirty jacket tails, muttered, 'Gracious me!' then brushed them clean. When they were clean, he let them fall back to the ground, whereupon they soon got dirty again, so he picked them up once more, muttered another 'Gracious me!' and brushed them all over again.

Kasper watched Jingo in amazement for a while, then looked round the alleyway.

The City doesn't look very sparkling, thought Kasper. All I can see at the moment are leaking drainpipes, broken windows and piles of rubbish. And this alleyway smells revolting. It needs a good dose of bleach and disinfectant.

'And now, Master Kasper,' began Jingo, his voice bubbling with excitement, 'it's my turn to surprise you.'

'It is?' said Kasper.

'Have you any idea who I'm going to cook the pie for?'

'None at all.'

'Master Kasper,' he said 'you are holding the ingredients that will make the favourite pie of …' And here he took a deep breath so he could say it loudly and with pride, 'The King.'

'The King?' said Kasper. 'The King of what?'

'The King of The Gloom, of course,' Jingo replied. 'KING STREETWISE!' And his voice echoed up and down the alley.

'STREETWISE … TREETWISE … REETWISE … EETWISE … TWISE … WISE … ISE … SSSSS.'

*Kasper and the Glitter*
Philip Ridley

*Text © 1994, Philip Ridley; illustrations © 2008, Moreno Chiacchiera/Beehive Illustration.*

## Reader guides

# Unhelpful sentences

■ Look at these sentences. They are difficult to read. Can you rewrite them using punctuation to make them more readable?

mum said its very cold I quite agree said gran

our teacher said playtime great said shaun lets get the football

the cows said moo good morning the farmer shouted

the clock says eight o clock said my mum I'd better be going

my gran said she was feeling fit give you a race I said OK she replied

put your coat on mum said why I moaned because I say so she said

the forecast said it could rain joe said I hope it doesn't I replied

lisa said she was bored and danny said lets go out on bikes

Name:

## Reader guides

# Pick an argument

■ Cut out these strips and pick an argument.

Two people arguing over which one of them was the first to get to the supermarket checkout.

A mum arguing with her child who is being really stroppy in a cafe.

A hare arguing with a tortoise about which one of them would win a race.

A driving instructor telling his pupil off for driving so badly and the pupil disagreeing.

A pot arguing with a saucepan about which of them is the most useful.

A dog arguing with its owner that the walk they just went on was too short.

PHOTOCOPIABLE **SCHOLASTIC**
www.scholastic.co.uk

# Audiences and sentences

## Objective

Review and edit sentences with reference to the audience of a text.

## Background knowledge

The audience of an act of communication has a lot of influence upon the way people speak and write. Considerations will include:

● **The anticipated response of the reader to a text:** Acts of communication are worded in specific ways according to their purpose. Words are selected that match whatever the reader or hearer is expected to do in response to the words. For example, will they persuade them to buy something?

● **The identity of the reader:** People speak differently to people of different ages or levels of understanding of a subject. The complexity of sentences and vocabulary used will vary depending on who the anticipated audience of a text is.

● **The relationship between the parties to the communication:** In linguistics this is referred to as the 'tenor' of an act of communication. People will sometimes address their boss in a different way to how they address their friends. The relationship between two people will determine the level of formality used and the tone of the written or spoken exchange.

## Activities

These activities provide a chance to reflect upon audience and sentences used in specific contexts. Children learn a lot about this area in undertaking their own writing activities for a variety of audiences.

● **Photocopiable page 140 'Sentence types and text types'**
Children need to separate sentences from two different texts. As they are undertaking the activity, you can ask them how they are telling the sentences apart.

● **Photocopiable page 141 'Formal and informal'**
Two types of sentence are shown together, each saying a similar thing, but one written in a more formal style than

the other. Once they have grouped the two different sets of sentences, children can revisit the two groups, observing what sort of vocabulary differentiates the two types of communication.

● **Photocopiable page 142 'Rhyming slang'**
Through playing with the inventiveness of a particular dialect, children can engage with the richness of non-standard dialects. This activity can provide an opportunity to discuss non-standard variations in the language, noticing that the genius of rhyming slang lay in its development as a furtive means of communication in a particular context.

## Further ideas

● **Relaxed and formal dialogue:** As a drama activity children can work in pairs devising either an informal situation into which they inject formal dialogue, or a formal situation that they act out with informal speech.

● **Television exchanges:** Make a tape recording of a selection of one-minute exchanges of dialogue from various programmes on the television (copyright permitting). Listen to the exchanges and ask the children to discuss the relationship between the participants and how that is reflected in the language. Focus upon two questions: What is the relationship between these people? How does that show in the way they speak to each other? There should be noticeable differences between, for example, a family in a situation comedy, a chat show and an interview on the news.

● **Card game instructions:** Children can read through instructions for games and try writing their own examples.

## What's on the CD-ROM

On the CD-ROM you will find:
● Printable versions of all three photocopiable pages.
● Answers to 'Sentence types and text types' and 'Formal and informal'.
● Interactive versions of 'Sentence types and text types' and 'Formal and informal'.

Name:

# Sentence types and text types

■ Cut out the boxes below.

■ Some of them belong to the instructions for a game. Some of them belong to a joke.

■ Collect the sentences from each type of text. Try rebuilding the two texts.

| | |
|---|---|
| A man was walking down the road and he saw a woman taking a dog for a walk. | And the woman said "That's true – but this isn't my dog." |
| Hold your cards face downwards so that nobody can see them – not even you. | He said "Hello" and she says "Hello" back. So he asked "Does your dog bite?" and the woman said "No." |
| Deal the whole pack of cards between the players. | Take turns to place one card face upwards in the middle of the group. |
| The man bent over and patted the dog and the dog snapped at him and sunk its teeth into his hand. | The man jumped up and down screaming "I thought you said your dog doesn't bite." |
| To win the game a player must be the first to notice this, place a hand on the cards and shout "Snap!" | If a card is placed in the pile that bears the same number of pips or picture as the card already in the middle then it is a 'Snap'. |

**Audiences and sentences**

# Formal and informal

■  The boxes below contain sentences saying similar things.
■  Can you match one sentence with another, pairing the sentences saying similar things?
■  Decide which one is more formal and which one is less formal.

| | |
|---|---|
| I find your behaviour inappropriate. | That telly programme was great. |
| I enjoyed the television programme immensely. | Please depart. |
| Can I go to the loo? | Would it be possible for me to use the bathroom? |
| Thank you for inviting me to your abode. | I don't like the way you're behaving. |
| Thanks for asking me round to your house. | Stop doing that. |
| Go away. | I'd love another plate of pudding. |
| There is an unappealing odour in this room. | The room smells horrible. |
| I would greatly enjoy a further helping of the sweet course. | I would appreciate it if you would desist. |

Name:

# Rhyming slang

Rhyming slang is a part of the cockney dialect of East London. It started with speakers using a way of communicating without being understood by people who may have been checking up on them. You may have a similar way of communicating with your friends, using secret words for certain things. It has a brilliant way of working.

1. The start word

2. is rhymed with another word.

3. This rhyming word is now used.

Captain Cook

I'm reading this Captain Cook

Sometimes another word linked to the rhyming word is used.

My mate.

My china plate.

Hello, me old china!

■ Try inventing your own rhyming-slang terms and putting them in a sentence.

| Sentence | Explanation |
|---|---|
| I saw my animal at the pool. | animal = creature – rhymes with teacher, pool rhymes with school, so 'I saw my teacher at the school' |
| | |
| | |
| | |

**PHOTOCOPIABLE**

Illustrations © 2008, Moreno Chiacchiera/Beehive Illustration.

# Writing speech

## Objective

Accurately and imaginatively present speech in writing.

## Writing focus

The writing focus of this chapter turns children towards the resource of their own speech and the words spoken by those around them, as well as imaginative examples from stories and events. Speech marking and writing cannot be effectively learned without first generating some real and lively subject matter.

## Skills to writing

● **Tuned to speech**

Keep the whole class tuned to the different ways in which certain things are said. At some point there came a tendency for the command *Be quiet* to be reworded by teenagers as *Talk to the hand*. Changes and additions like these should be gathered and children should be encouraged to be speech investigators, listening out for the ways of saying something that are particular to an age group or locality.

● **Drama**

There is an integral link between the effective teaching of speech marks and drama. Of course, it's not just about punctuation. It's also about content. As part of the process of devising and demarcating conversations, children need to have them. They need to act out the persuasion of a teacher, nagging of a parent, arguing, whinging, sneering and sweet talking, that will form the dialogue in their texts.

● **Punctuation to speech**

One of the principles of this chapter – and book – is that punctuation makes texts work better. One way of exploring this is by working with children on the punctuation of any text they have been asked to read aloud. In the *Kasper and the Glitter* example on photocopiable page 136 'Helping the reader', the text of

the paragraph commencing with *Now that Jingo didn't have a basket…* is a good example of a paragraph that is hard to read without its commas. Commas tell the reader how to split the long sentence – useful for pauses and breaths when reading aloud. At speech marks a reader can inflect their voice, as if becoming the speaker. Question and exclamation marks guide in how certain sentences should be said.

● **Conversations aloud**

When reading texts with speech in them, encourage the class to occasionally use the text as a script, figuring out which lines belong to which speaker and then having individuals take their role. Children become better attuned to the liveliness of speech in text when they hear the lines turned into a conversation.

● **Quotations**

Reported speech isn't just the reserve of narrative writing. It has a clear part to play in recount texts but can also figure in every other text type. If you read a popular science book, it's not uncommon to find the pages spiced up with small quotations from the scientists whose ideas populate the pages. As children write their explanation and report texts, they can be encouraged to listen out for interesting lines to quote in their text from whatever resources stimulate their writing. To prevent whole paragraph copying, suggest that quotes do need to be short, one-sentence items. Also make it clear that good quotes are sharp, memorable lines.

## Activities

● **Photocopiable page 145 'Tapes and transcripts'**

In this activity, children tape and use speech as a starting point for writing. They will need practice with the idea of transcribing speech word for word but, once they have done this, can produce the comparative forms.

● **Photocopiable page 146 'Scrambling eggs'**

One feature of writing children need to attune to is the difference between more formally written texts and the less formal nature of most speech. To attune children to the difference between formal writing and the way we say things, this recipe adopts a verbose and formal style. Children have to puzzle out what each of the spaces is referring to and transpose this into regular ways of saying things.

## Write on

● **Character talk**

Use talk as a way of developing characters in narrative writing. Ask the children to try to put the things we need to know about a character into their speech. If they have a guilty secret, don't have the writer tell us in a plain sentence (*Josh was really a robot*). Have the character confess (*Josh said, 'Mum, there's something you should know'*). While doing this, characters can also be given a catchphrase or some other verbal feature.

● **One-line speech**

Children will often write speech in big chunks, unlike the exchange that would normally take place between two people. This activity explores the more interactive nature of conversation. Ask children to think of a context in which two people would have a discussion – be it informative, argumentative or moaning. Whatever the content, ask them to span the conversation over a page, using short lines rather than big paragraphs of speech. One character must interrupt or question the other.

● **Argument**

Children like writing arguments. They have usually been in or near one recently and can recall how they go. These can provide a good resource for a link to history, asking children to write the sharp exchange that will have taken place between characters from the history topic they are studying.

● **Soap opera**

Many children at this age will watch a soap opera and this can provide a great stimulus for thinking about, and writing, speech. Ask the children to devise a street of houses or block of flats and think of the characters that could live there, then to imagine some tensions that could exist between them. Having done this, they can either write conversations between these characters as dialogue or produce a playscript.

### What's on the CD-ROM

On the CD-ROM you will find:
● Printable versions of both photocopiable pages.
● Answers to 'Scrambling eggs'.

**Writing speech**

# Tapes and transcripts

■ Make a tape recording of someone telling you a true short story about themselves. Listen to the tape and find a section that is really interesting in the story. In the box marked Transcript, copy out what they said, word for word. In the box marked Written sentences, put the words they use into written sentences. What sorts of changes do you make to their words?

| Transcript | Written sentences |
|---|---|
| | |

Name:

# Writing speech

# Scrambling eggs

■ Look at these complicated sentences from an instructional text. Look up any words you don't understand in a dictionary.

■ Can you alter the sentences to make them easier to understand? Try rewriting the recipe so that someone younger than you could understand it.

| Original | Rewrite |
|---|---|
| To manufacture scrambled eggs: | |
| Commence by shattering two eggs into a bowl. | |
| Cudgel the eggs thoroughly by operating a whisk. | |
| Aggregate a little milk into the mixture. | |
| Liquefy margarine in a frying pan. | |
| Gently decant the egg mixture into the pan and stir to scramble. | |
| Purvey the eggs, on toast if you elect. | |

**PHOTOCOPIABLE**

# Subject knowledge

## 1. Preliminary notes about grammar

Grammar involves the way in which words of different types are combined into sentences. The explanatory sections that follow will include definitions of types of word along with notes on how they are combined into sentences.

Three preliminary points about grammar:

● Function is all-important. Where a word is placed in relation to another word is crucial in deciding whether it is functioning as a verb or a noun. For example, the word 'run' will often be thought of as a verb. However, in a sentence like *They went for a run*, the word functions as a noun and the verb is 'went'.

● There are some consistencies in the way spelling is linked to grammar. For example, words like 'play' and 'shout' have the '-ed' ending to make past tense verbs, 'played' and 'shouted'. Adjectives like 'quick' and 'slow' take a '-ly' ending to make adverbs like 'quickly' and 'slowly'. There are exceptions to these rules but such consistencies can still prove useful when it comes to understanding the grammar of sentences.

● Nothing is sacred in language. Rules change over time; the double negative has gained currency and regional variation in accent and dialect is now far more valued than has been the case in the past. The rules of grammar that follow are subject to change as the language we use lives and grows.

## 2. Words and functions

Grammar picks out the functions of words. The major classes or types of word in the English language are:

### Noun

The name of something or someone, including concrete things, such as 'dog' or 'tree', and abstract things, such as 'happiness' or 'fear'.

### Pronoun

A word that replaces a noun. The noun 'John' in *John is ill* can be replaced by a pronoun 'he', making *He is ill*.

### Verb

A word that denotes an action or a happening. In the sentence *I ate the cake* the verb is 'ate'. These are sometimes referred to as 'doing' words.

### Adjective

A word that modifies a noun. In the phrase *the little boat* the adjective 'little' describes the noun 'boat'.

**Adverb**

A word that modifies a verb. In the phrase *he slowly walked* the adverb is 'slowly'.

**Preposition**

A word or phrase that shows the relationship of one thing to another. In the phrase *the house beside the sea* the preposition 'beside' places the two nouns in relation to each other.

**Conjunction**

A word or phrase that joins other words and phrases. A simple example is the word 'and' that joins nouns in *Snow White and Doc and Sneezy*.

**Article**

The indefinite articles in English are 'a' and 'an' and the definite article is 'the'. Articles appear before nouns and denote whether the noun is specific (*give me the book*) or not (*give me a book*).

**Interjection**

A word or phrase expressing or exclaiming an emotion, such as 'Oh!' and 'Aaargh!'
The various word types can be found in the following example sentences:

| Lou | saw | his | new | house | from | the | train. |
|---|---|---|---|---|---|---|---|
| noun | verb | pronoun | adjective | noun | preposition | article | noun |
| Yeow! | I | hit | my | head | on | the | door. |
| interjection | pronoun | verb | pronoun | noun | preposition | article | noun |
| Amir | sadly | lost | his | bus fare | down | the | drain. |
| noun | adverb | verb | pronoun | noun | preposition | article | noun |
| Give | Jan | a | good | book | for | her | birthday. |
| verb | noun | article | adjective | noun | conjunction | pronoun | noun |

The pages that follow provide more information on these word classes.

**Nouns**

There are four types of noun in English.

**Common nouns** are general names for things. For example, in the sentence *I fed the dog*, the noun 'dog' could be used to refer to any dog, not to a specific one. Other examples include 'boy', 'country', 'book', 'apple'.

**Proper nouns** are the specific names given to identify things or people. In a phrase like *Sam is my dog* the word 'dog' is the common noun but 'Sam' is a proper noun because it refers to and identifies a specific dog. Other examples include 'the Prime Minister', 'Wales' and 'Amazing Grace'.

> A **noun** is the name of someone or something.

**Collective nouns** refer to a group of things together, such as 'a flock (of sheep)' or 'a bunch (of bananas)'.

**Abstract nouns** refer to things that are not concrete, such as an action, a concept, an event, quality or state. Abstract nouns like 'happiness' and 'fulfilment' refer to ideas or feelings which are uncountable; others, such as 'hour', 'joke' and 'quantity' are countable.

**Nouns** can be singular or plural. To change a singular to a plural the usual rule is to add 's'. This table includes other rules to bear in mind, however:

| If the singular ends in: | Rule | Examples |
|---|---|---|
| 'y' after a consonant | Remove 'y', add 'ies' | party → parties |
| 'y' after a vowel | add 's' | donkey → donkeys |
| 'o' after a consonant | add 'es' | potato → potatoes |
| 'o' after a vowel | add 's' | video → videos |
| an 's' sound such as 's', 'sh', 'x', 'z' | add 'es' | kiss → kisses<br>dish → dishes |
| a 'ch' sound such as 'ch' or 'tch' | add 'es' | watch → watches<br>church → churches |

### Pronouns

There are different classes of pronoun. The main types are:

**Personal pronouns** refer to people or things, such as 'I', 'you', 'it'. The personal pronouns distinguish between subject and object case ('I/me', 'he/ him', 'she/her', 'we/us', 'they/them' and the archaic 'thou/thee').

> A **pronoun** is a word that stands in for a noun.

**Reflexive pronouns** refer to people or things that are also the subject of the sentence. In the sentence *You can do this yourself* the pronoun 'yourself' refers to 'you'. Such pronouns end with '-self' or '-selves'. Other examples include 'myself', 'themselves'.

**Possessive pronouns** identify people or things as belonging to a person or thing. For example, in the sentence *The book is hers* the possessive pronoun 'hers' refers to 'the book'. Other examples include 'its' and 'yours'. Note that possessive pronouns never take an apostrophe.

**Relative pronouns** link relative clauses to their nouns. In the sentence *The man who was in disguise sneaked into the room* the relative clause 'who was in disguise' provides extra information about 'the man'. This relative clause is linked by the relative pronoun 'who'. Other examples include 'whom', 'which' and 'that'.

**Interrogative pronouns** are used in questions. They refer to the thing that is being asked about. In the question *What is your name?* and *Where is the book?* the pronouns 'what' and 'where' stand for the answers – the name and the location of the book.

**Demonstrative pronouns** are pronouns that 'point'. They are used to show the relation of the speaker to an object. There are four demonstrative pronouns in English 'this', 'that', 'these', 'those' used as in *This is my house* and *That is your house*. They have specific uses, depending upon the position of the object to the speaker:

|  | **Near to speaker** | **Far away from speaker** |
|---|---|---|
| **Singular** | this | that |
| **Plural** | these | those |

**Indefinite pronouns** stand in for an indefinite noun. The indefinite element can be the number of elements or the nature of them but they are summed up in ambiguous pronouns such as 'any', 'some' or 'several'. Other examples are the pronouns that end with '-body', '-one' and '-thing', such as 'somebody', 'everyone' and 'anything'.

### Person
Personal, reflexive and possessive pronouns can be in the first, second or third person.
- First-person pronouns ('I', 'we') involve the speaker or writer.
- Second-person pronouns ('you') refer to the listener or reader.
- Third-person pronouns refer to something other than these two participants in the communication ('he', 'she', 'it', 'they').

The person of the pronoun will agree with particular forms of verbs: 'I like'/'she likes'.

### Verbs
The **tense** of a verb places a happening in time. The main three tenses are the present, past and future.

To express an action that will take place in the future, verbs appear with 'will' or 'shall' (or 'going to'). The regular past tense is formed by the addition of the suffix '-ed', although some of the most common verbs in English (the 'strong' verbs) have irregular past tenses.

> A **verb** is a word that denotes an action or a happening.

| **Present tense (happening now)** | **Past tense (happened in past)** | **Future tense (to happen in future)** |
|---|---|---|
| am, say, find, kick | was, said, found, kicked | will be, will say, shall find, shall kick |

### Continuous verbs
The present participle form of a verb is used to show a continuous action. Whereas a past tense like 'kicked' denotes an action that happened ('I kicked'), the present participle denotes the action as happening and continuing as it is described (*I was kicking*, the imperfect tense, or *I am kicking*, the present continuous). There is a sense in these uses of an action that has not ended.

The present participle usually ends in '-ing', such as 'walking', 'finding', and continuous verbs are made with a form of the verb 'be', such as 'was' or 'am': *I was running* and *I am running*.

## Auxiliary verbs

Auxiliary verbs 'help' other verbs – they regularly accompany full verbs, always preceding them in a verb phrase. The auxiliary verbs in English can be divided into three categories:

**Primary verbs** are used to indicate the timing of a verb, such as 'be', 'have' or 'did' (including all their variations such as 'was', 'were', 'has', 'had' and so on). These can be seen at work in verb forms like *I was watching a film*, *He has finished eating*, *I didn't lose my keys*.

**Modal verbs** indicate the possibility of an action occurring or the necessity of it happening, such as *I might watch a film*, *I should finish eating* and *I shouldn't lose my keys*.

The modal verbs in English are: 'would', 'could', 'might', 'should', 'can', 'will', 'shall', 'may', and 'must'. These verbs never function on their own as main verbs. They always act as auxiliaries helping other verbs.

**Marginal modals**, namely 'dare', 'need', 'ought to' and 'used to'. These act as modals, such as in the sentences *I dared enter the room*, *You need to go away* and *I ought to eat my dinner*, but they can also act as main verbs, as in *I need cake*.

## Adjectives

The main function of adjectives is to define quality or quantity. Examples of the use of descriptions of quality include 'good story', 'sad day' and 'stupid dog'. Examples of the use of descriptions of quantity include 'some stories', 'ten days' and 'many dogs'.

> An **adjective** is a word that modifies a noun.

Adjectives can appear in one of three different degrees of intensity. In the table on page 152 it can be seen that there are '-er' and '-est' endings that show an adjective is comparative or superlative, though, as can be seen, there are exceptions. The regular comparative is formed by the addition of the suffix '-er' to shorter words and 'more' to longer words ('kind/kinder', 'beautiful/more beautiful'). The regular superlative is formed by the addition of the suffix '-est' to shorter words and 'most' to longer words. Note, however, that some common adjectives have irregular comparatives and superlatives.

| Nominative | Comparative | Superlative |
|---|---|---|
| The nominative is the plain form that describes a noun. | The comparative implies a comparison between the noun and something else. | The superlative is the ultimate degree of a particular quality. |
| **Examples**<br>long<br>small<br>big<br>fast<br>bad<br>good<br>far | **Examples**<br>longer<br>smaller<br>bigger<br>faster<br>worse<br>better<br>farther/further | **Examples**<br>longest<br>smallest<br>biggest<br>fastest<br>worst<br>best<br>farthest/furthest |

## Adverbs

Adverbs provide extra information about the time, place or manner in which a verb happened.

> An **adverb** is a word that modifies a verb.

| Manner<br>Provides information about the manner in which the action was done. | Ali *quickly* ran home.<br>The cat climbed *fearfully* up the tree. |
|---|---|
| Time<br>Provides information about the time at which the action occurred. | *Yesterday* Ali ran home.<br>*Sometimes* the cat climbed up the tree. |
| Place<br>Provides information about where the action took place. | *Outside* Ali ran home.<br>*In the garden* the cat climbed up the tree. |

Variations in the degree of intensity of an adverb are indicated by other adjectives such as 'very', 'rather', 'quite' and 'somewhat'. Comparative forms include 'very quickly', 'rather slowly', and 'most happily'.

The majority of single-word adverbs are made by adding '-ly' to an adjective: 'quick/quickly', 'slow/slowly' and so on.

## Prepositions

Prepositions show how nouns or pronouns are positioned in relation to other nouns and pronouns in the same sentence. This can often be the location of one thing in relation to another in space, such as 'on', 'over', 'near'; or time, such as 'before', 'after'.

Prepositions are usually placed before a noun. They can consist of one word (*The cat* in *the tree...*), two words (*The cat* close to *the gate...*) or three (*The cat* on top of *the roof...*).

> A **preposition** is a word or phrase that shows the relationship of one thing to another.

## Connectives

The job of a connective is to maintain cohesion through a piece of text.

> A **connective** is a word or phrase that links clauses or sentences.

Connectives can be:
- Conjunctions – connect clauses within one sentence.
- Connecting adverbs – connect ideas in separate sentences.

## Conjunctions

Conjunctions are a special type of connective. There are two types: coordinating or subordinating.

**Coordinating conjunctions** connect clauses of equal weight. For example: *I like cake and I like tea.* Coordinating conjunctions include: 'and', 'but', 'or' and 'so'.

**Subordinating conjunctions** are used where the clauses of unequal weight, they begin a subordinate clause. For example: *The dog barked because he saw the burglar.* Subordinating conjunctions include: 'because', 'when', 'while', 'that', 'although', 'if', 'until', 'after', before' and 'since'.

| Name of conjunction | Nature of conjunction | Examples |
|---|---|---|
| Addition | One or more clause together | We had our tea *and* went out to play. |
| Opposition | One or more clauses in opposition | I like coffee *but* my brother hates it. It could rain *or* it could snow. |
| Time | One or more clauses connected over time | Toby had his tea *then* went out to play. The bus left *before* we reached the stop. |
| Cause | One or more clauses causing or caused by another | I took a map *so that* we wouldn't get lost. We got lost *because* we had the wrong map. |

## Connecting adverbs

The table below provides the function of the adverbs and examples of the type of words used for that purpose.

| | |
|---|---|
| Addition | 'also', 'furthermore', 'moreover', 'likewise' |
| Opposition | 'however', 'never the less', 'on the other hand' |
| Time | 'just then', 'meanwhile', 'later' |
| Result | 'therefore', 'as a result' |
| Reinforcing | 'besides', 'anyway' |
| Explaining | 'for example', 'in other words' |
| Listing | 'first of all', 'finally' |

# 3. Understanding sentences

## Types of sentence

The four main types of sentence are declarative, interrogative, imperative and exclamatory. The function of a sentence has an effect on the word order; imperatives, for example, often begin with a verb.

## Sentences: Clauses and complexities

### Phrases

A phrase is a set of words performing a grammatical function. In the sentence *The little, old, fierce dog brutally chased the sad and fearful cat*, there are three distinct units performing grammatical functions. The first phrase in this sentence essentially names the dog and provides descriptive information. This is a noun phrase, performing the job of a noun – 'the little, old, fierce dog'. To do this the phrase uses adjectives.

| Sentence type | Function | Examples |
|---|---|---|
| Declarative | Makes a statement | The house is down the lane. Joe rode the bike. |
| Interrogative | Asks a question | Where is the house? What is Joe doing? |
| Imperative | Issues a command or direction | Turn left at the traffic lights. Get on your bike! |
| Exclamatory | Issues an interjection | Wow, what a mess! Oh no! |

The important thing to look out for is the way in which words build around a key word in a phrase. So here the words 'little', 'old' and 'fierce' are built around the word 'dog'. In examples like these, 'dog' is referred to as the **headword** and the adjectives are termed **modifiers**. Together, the modifier and headword make up the noun phrase. Modifiers can also come after the noun, as in *The little, old, fierce dog that didn't like cats brutally chased the sad and fearful cat*. In this example 'little, 'old' and 'fierce' are **premodifiers** and the phrase 'that didn't like cats' is a **postmodifier**.

| Phrase type | Examples |
|---|---|
| Noun phrase | The *little, old fierce dog* didn't like cats. She gave him *a carefully and colourfully covered book*. |
| Verb phrase | The dog *had been hiding* in the house. The man *climbed through* the window without a sound. |
| Adjectival phrase | The floor was *completely clean*. The floor was *so clean you could eat your dinner off it*. |
| Adverbial phrase | I finished my lunch *very slowly indeed*. *More confidently than usual*, she entered the room. |
| Prepositional phrase | The cat sat *at the top of* the tree. The phone rang *in the middle of* the night. |

The noun phrase is just one of the types of phrase that can be made.

Notice that phrases can appear within phrases. A noun phrase like 'carefully and colourfully covered book' contains the adjectival phrase 'carefully and colourfully covered'. This string of words forms the adjectival phrase in which the words 'carefully' and 'colourfully' modify the adjective 'covered'. Together these words, 'carefully and colourfully covered', modify the noun 'book', creating a distinct noun phrase. This is worth noting as it shows how the boundaries between phrases can be blurred – a fact that can cause confusion unless borne in mind!

### Clauses

Clauses are units of meaning included within a sentence, usually containing a verb and other elements linked to it. *The burglar ran* is a clause containing the definite article, noun and verb; *The burglar quickly ran from the little house* is also a clause that adds an adverb, preposition and adjective. The essential element in a clause is the verb. Clauses look very much like small sentences, indeed sentences can be constructed of just one clause: *The burglar hid*, *I like cake*.

Sentences can also be constructed out of a number of clauses linked together: *The burglar ran and I chased him because he stole my cake*. This sentence contains three clauses: 'The burglar ran', 'I chased him', 'he stole my cake'.

### Clauses and phrases: the difference

Clauses include participants in an action denoted by a verb. Phrases, however, need not necessarily contain a verb. These phrases make little sense on their own: 'without a sound', 'very slowly indeed'. They work as part of a clause.

### Simple, compound and complex sentences

The addition of clauses can make complex or compound sentences.

**Simple sentences** are made up of one clause, for example: *The dog barked*, *Sam was scared*.

**Compound sentences** are made up of clauses added to clauses. In compound sentences each of the clauses is of equal value; no clause is dependent on another. An example of a compound sentence is: *The dog barked and the parrot squawked*. Both these clauses are of equal importance: 'The dog barked', 'the parrot squawked'. Other compound sentences include, for example: *I like coffee and I like chocolate*, *I like coffee, but I don't like tea*.

**Complex sentences** are made up of a main clause with a subordinate clause or clauses. Subordinate clauses make sense in relation to the main clause. They say something about it and are dependent upon it, such as in the sentences: *The dog barked because he saw a burglar*; *Sam was scared so he phoned the police*.

In both these cases the subordinate clause ('he saw a burglar', 'he phoned the police') is elaborating on the main clause. They explain why the dog barked or why Sam was scared and, in doing so, are subordinate to those actions. The reader needs to see the main clauses to fully appreciate what the subordinate ones are stating.

## Subject and object

The **subject** of a sentence or clause is the agent that performs the action denoted by the verb – *Shaun threw the ball*. The **object** is the agent to which the verb is done – 'ball'. It could be said that the subject does the verb to the object (a simplification but a useful one). The simplest type of sentence is known as the SVO (subject–verb–object) sentence (or clause), as in *You lost your way*, *I found the book* and *Lewis met Chloe*.

## The active voice and the passive voice

These contrast two ways of saying the same thing:

| Active voice | Passive voice |
|---|---|
| I found the book.<br>Megan met Ben.<br>The cow jumped over the moon. | The book was found by me.<br>Ben was met by Megan.<br>The moon was jumped over by the cow. |

The two types of clause put the same subject matter in a different voice. Passive clauses are made up of a subject and verb followed by an agent.

| The book | was found by | me. |
|---|---|---|
| subject | verb | agent |
| Ben | was met by | Megan. |
| subject | verb | agent |

Sentences can be written in the active or the passive voice. A sentence can be changed from the active to the passive voice by:
- moving the subject to the end of the clause
- moving the object to the start of the clause
- changing the verb or verb phrase by placing a form of the verb 'be' before it (as in 'was found')
- changing the verb or verb phrase by placing 'by' after it.

In passive clauses the agent can be deleted, either because it does not need mentioning or because a positive choice is made to omit it. Texts on science may leave out the agent, with sentences such as *The water is added to the salt and stirred*.

## 4. Punctuation

Punctuation provides marks within sentences that guide the reader. Speech doesn't need punctuation (and would sound bizarre if it included noises for full stops and so on). In speech, much is communicated by pausing, changing tone and so on. In writing, the marks within and around a sentence provide indications of when to pause, when something is being quoted and so on.

| Punctuation | Uses | Examples |
|---|---|---|
| A | **Capital letter**<br>1. Start a sentence.<br>2. Indicate proper nouns.<br>3. Emphasise certain words. | All I want is cake.<br>You can call me Al.<br>I want it TOMORROW! |
| • | **Full stop**<br>Ends sentences that are not questions or exclamations. | This is a sentence. |
| ? | **Question mark**<br>Ends a sentence that is a question. | Is this a question? |
| ! | **Exclamation mark**<br>Ends a sentence that is an exclamation. | Don't do that! |
| " " ' ' | **Quotation (speech) marks (or inverted commas)**<br>Enclose direct speech. Can be double or single. | "Help me," the man yelled.<br>'Help me,' the man yelled. |
| , | **Comma**<br>1. Places a pause between clauses within a sentence.<br>2. Separates items in a list.<br>3. Separates adjectives in a series.<br>4. Completely encloses clauses inserted in a sentence.<br>5. Marks speech from words denoting who said them. | We were late, although it didn't matter.<br>You will need eggs, butter and flour.<br>I wore a long, green, frilly skirt.<br>We were, after we had rushed to get there, late for the film.<br>'Thank you,' I said. |
| — | **Hyphen**<br>Connects elements of certain words. | Co-ordinator, south-west. |
| : | **Colon**<br>1. Introduces lists (including examples). | To go skiing these are the main items you will need: a hat, goggles, gloves and sunscreen. |
| | 2. Introduces summaries. | We have learned the following on the ski slope: do a snow plough to slow down… |
| | 3. Introduces (direct) quotations. | My instructor always says: 'Bend those knees.' |
| | 4. Introduces a second clause that expands or illustrates the meaning of the first. | The snow hardened: it turned into ice. |

| Punctuation | Uses | Examples |
|---|---|---|
| **;** | **Semicolon**<br>1.  Separates two closely linked clauses, and shows there is a link between them.<br>2.  Separates items in a complex list. | On Tuesday, the bus was late; the train was early.<br><br>You can go by aeroplane, train and taxi; Channel tunnel train, coach, then a short walk; or aeroplane and car. |
| **'** | **Apostrophe of possession**<br>Denotes the ownership of one thing by another (see page 159). | This is Mona's scarf.<br>These are the teachers' books. |
| **'** | **Apostrophe of contraction**<br>Shows the omission of a letter(s) when two (or occasionally more) words are contracted. | Don't walk on the grass. |
| **...** | **Ellipsis**<br>1.  Shows the omission of words.<br><br>2.  Indicates a pause. | The teacher moaned, 'Look at this floor… a mess… this class…'<br>Lou said: 'I think I locked the door… no, hang on, did I?' |
| **( )** | **Brackets**<br>Contains a parenthesis – a word or phrase added to a sentence to give a bit more information. | The cupboard (which had been in my family for years) was broken. |
| **—** | **Dash**<br>1.  Indicates additional information, with more emphasis than a comma.<br>2.  Indicates a pause, especially for effect at the end of a sentence.<br>3.  Contains extra information (used instead of brackets). | She is a teacher – and a very good one too.<br>We all know what to expect – the worst.<br>You finished that job – and I don't know how – before the deadline. |

## Adding an apostrophe of possession

The addition of an apostrophe can create confusion. The main thing to look at is the noun – ask:

- Is it singular or plural?
- Does it end in an 's'?

| If the noun is singular and doesn't end in 's', you add an apostrophe and an 's', for example:<br>Indra's house<br>the firefighter's bravery | If the noun is singular and ends in 's', you add an apostrophe and an 's', for example:<br>the bus's wheels<br>Thomas's pen |
| --- | --- |
| If the noun is plural and doesn't end in 's', you add an apostrophe and an 's', for example:<br>the women's magazine<br>the geese's flight | If the noun is plural and ends in 's', you add an apostrophe but don't add an 's', for example:<br>the boys' clothes<br>the dancers' performance |

# Further reading

Carter, R; Goddard, A; Reah, D; Sanger, K; Bowring, K (2001) *Working with Texts: A Core Book for Language Analysis* (second edition), Routledge

Crystal, D (2004) *Rediscover Grammar* (second edition), Longman

Crystal, D (2003) *The Cambridge Encyclopedia of the English Language* (second edition), Cambridge University Press
A big volume but very accessible, covering many areas of English including grammar, punctuation and dialect. Filled with interesting asides and examples from sources as varied as Shakespeare to Monty Python.

Hurford, JR (1994) *Grammar: A Student's Guide*, Cambridge University Press
An excellent text, setting out basic guidelines on the workings of grammar.

Sealey, A (1996) *Learning About Language: Issues for Primary Teachers*, Open University Press
A more theoretical work that presents some of the issues and arguments surrounding knowledge about language.

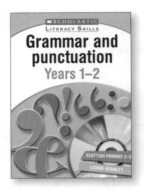

# SCHOLASTIC

## Also available in this series:

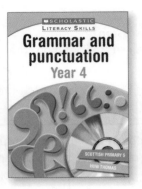
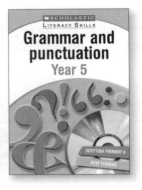
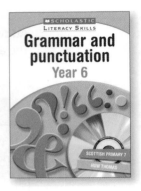

ISBN 978-1407-10045-6    ISBN 978-1407-10046-3    ISBN 978-1407-10047-0    ISBN 978-1407-10048-7    ISBN 978-1407-10049-4

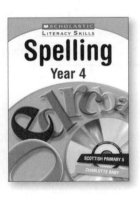

ISBN 978-1407-10055-5    ISBN 978-1407-10056-2    ISBN 978-1407-10057-9    ISBN 978-1407-10058-6    ISBN 978-1407-10059-3

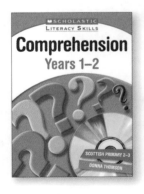
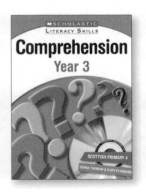
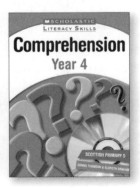
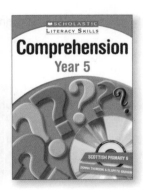
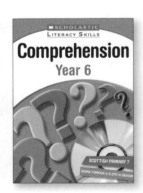

ISBN 978-1407-10050-0    ISBN 978-1407-10051-7    ISBN 978-1407-10052-4    ISBN 978-1407-10053-1    ISBN 978-1407-10054-8

To find out more, call: 0845 603 9091
or visit our website www.scholastic.co.uk